ABC&D

CREATING A REGENERATIVE CIRCULAR ECONOMY FOR ALL

*A is for apple; a source of knowledge and life while **B** is for a basic dividend and the autonomy it brings. **C** is for a circular economy, creating and circulating value and **D** is for democracy reimagined for our 21st Century*

Ken Webster & Craig Johnson

First Edition published in 2021
by TerraPreta Publishing. Enquiries to:
publishing@terra-preta.co.uk

ISBN 978-0-9559831-3-9
Editorial: *Catherine Broadhead*
Cover design and book layout: *Debs Oakes*
Book illustrations: *Graham Pritchard*
POD Printed on demand by IngramSpark™ 2021. Price £27.99

Every effort has been made to ensure that URLs are correct at time of
going to press. If any copyright holders have been overlooked the publisher
will be pleased to include any necessary credits in subsequent reprints and
additions.

Notes and Exceptions for use of the Images
In creating the book illustrations by Graham Pritchard, we set out to
produce a unique library of graphics for circular economy communications - to be used and shared beyond the publication of this book. Each
pictogram is built on combinations and sections of circles. This represents
the qualities of circular economy by creating our own 'eco-system' of visual
elements. This standardised approach is inspired by the ISOTYPE movement. Objects such as trees, animals, vehicles and even landscapes are
created in this way, with only a few unavoidable exceptions. Schematics of
circular economy systems use flowing fine lines to link the subjects. These
Illustrations may be purchased at high resolution for use specified at
www.terra-preta.co.uk.

CONTENTS

01

THE IMAGINARY INTRODUCED

Through seven episodes the imaginary uncovers a Worldview; Economies are revealed; then Economies are changed and our ideas about them too. The story of the new economy needs to be based within: a 'systems' framework; the digital data and its tools; the abundance and diversity of the earth's endowment; the world's distributed renewable energy sources; the re-invention of money; and an appreciation of and access to the historical and ongoing 'commons'.

02

THE FOOD SYSTEM OF OUR FUTURE – THE ENABLING CONDITIONS

The system conditions shape the outcome. The paradox of food, diet and health is that without access to tools, resources, infrastructure and effective income and currency (including credit) it is hard to see how food futures can improve for the majority of people.

03

REGENERATIVE FARMING – THE SEARCH FOR DREAM FARM NETWORK 1.0

How 'waste=food' and the other principles of the materials economy relate to food and farming systems. Principles of the circular economy working at farm scale. Regenerative food enterprise networks introduced – individual regenerative farm and food enterprises cannot succeed in isolation.

04

REGENERATIVE FOOD ENTERPRISE NETWORKS – 3D APPLE ORCHARDS AND OCEAN FARMS

Think network, not just farm. 'Nested markets' and a tri-centric governance model for food system transformation. The 'partner state' as shaper and creator of markets and facilitator for local people to engage with their local 'food commons'. Healthy growth is about successful scaling out (not just scaling up) of regenerative enterprises within distributed local and regional food networks.

05

CITIES IN A CIRCULAR ECONOMY

What kind of circular economy in cities – a circular economy for transition or transformation? The question matters if we are headed for a new economic paradigm where the economy is more devolved, and one where the main questions are not about production so much as access and distribution. If urban economic development becomes more devolved, who controls the distribution and of what?

06

FOOD SYSTEMS IN CITIES

Some city food utopias revealed. For regenerative food systems to thrive in and around cities, it's a lot about 'wise governance' setting enabling conditions for: effective stocks, flows and exchanges of biological nutrients; regeneration of soil; money flows and exchanges; 'food commons' infrastructure and organisations; 'enterprise stacking'; and development of business enterprises with 21st century purpose.

07

...AND D IS FOR DEMOCRACY

An elementary duty of the democratic state is to create a minimum standard of life below which no human being can fall. Central to discussion of food systems and food sovereignty is a reinvigorated democracy – at its core this is about the potential for people to participate in creating their own well-being and to make decisions which matter. It is argued that a participatory democracy emerges from the basis of a security and confidence of having a universal basic dividend, an enabling macroeconomic framework and an inclusive, contemporary and scientific worldview.

CHAPTER 1

THE IMAGINARY INTRODUCED

"All our knowledge has its origins in our perceptions".
Leonardo da Vinci

Imagining is not science. Imagining, we argue, is part of creating that 'sense of direction' and meaning in a narrative which underlies social change. Often it constitutes the search for a coherent set of stories about human thought; how and why we make choices; how decisions are made in society; and how resources are used. Science can tell us whether these stories are more or less reasonable, whether they are connected to a contemporary sense of how the world actually works. However, science does not isolate the truth (although we grew up believing this to be the case) – it is just one of the best tools we have in a fluid, shifting world.

Writer Yuval Noah Harari[1] insists that change in society comes through the emergence of narratives that become acceptable rather than testable. Change requires these new narratives to be seen as better than the ones we have now. An obvious place to start is the idea of an economy.

It's time to get a bit closer to the economy as it is imagined now. The economists of the 19th and early 20th centuries were impressed by the physicists and went in search of parallel laws of economic relationships to those in physics. If they could find them then Economics would be the Queen of social science. If the physicists could drill down to fundamentals and use this analysis to understand, predict and control then why not apply a mechanistic lens to economics?

The economy, in an era of machines, is imagined to be a particular kind of machine. The individual firm or worker (or consumer) is a rational actor and accepts the discipline of the market since it gives the most efficient result. That is where equilibrium is found[2]. These individual decisions can be aggregated to describe an Economy. Big E.

The metaphor then switches slightly to Economy as engineered pipework. In the pipes is money. Money represents all those production and consumption exchanges. Prices are messages after all. It is an historical artefact that the economy is archetypally seen as being a system described by the circulation of money flows. Here is a familiar text book diagram, based on Paul Samuelson's best-selling 20th century book *Economics*.

Figure 1 (left): Reimagine the simple dandelion, often thought of as a weed due to being resilient and abundant; not only feeds the soil around it but also has a short season allowing other plants to thrive around it after dying back; flowers, even in the most difficult environments (cracks in pavements etc.). It is fantastic for bees and pollination, has medicinal properties, edible leaves and roots which can make a coffee substitute. The dandelion does all this with very little requirement on resources and using just the wind to carry its seeds effortlessley across what was once thought impossible distances – until science discovered that each seed creates its own vortex, in order to transport it across continents and beyond.

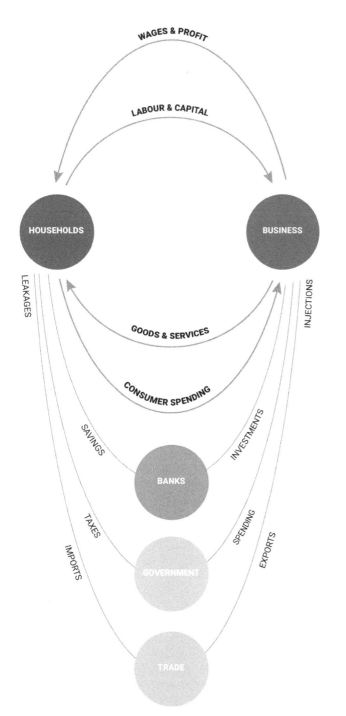

WAGES & PROFIT

LABOUR & CAPITAL

HOUSEHOLDS

BUSINESS

LEAKAGES

INJECTIONS

GOODS & SERVICES

CONSUMER SPENDING

SAVINGS

INVESTMENTS

BANKS

TAXES

SPENDING

IMPORTS

EXPORTS

GOVERNMENT

TRADE

Figure 2 (left): A simplified diagram of the economy based on: Paul Samuelson[56]

Illustration: Graham Pritchard

This pipework is a stylised closed loop of money in exchange. It is, unsurprisingly for engineering pipework, all valves and no leaks. Via the market, the interaction of supply and demand, there is general equilibrium in the long run. There has to be, it's pipework! There is nothing creative or indeterminate about it. This pipework is conceived to represent the economy, despite all that is apparently outside of it: despite no energy to drive it; despite the environment it depends upon; despite society, which gives it purpose and where the very existence of the long term seems troubling. Money is oil in the machine of exchange. Illusion indeed here, even if the mathematics are detailed and precise... now, the story goes, if only the people would fit the model then all would be well, since the economy is self-evidently successful because it produces more over time and is as efficient as can be. It's clearly a Utopia which depends on people fitting the machine, governments balancing budgets and the exchange rate balancing trade.

Oh? This arrangement can produce growth, apparently, from within: technology makes it all more efficient. But that seems to be mixing the metaphors... a self-growing pipework anyone?

Disappointment seems to wait at the corner. But it's simplifying reality, right? It's a snapshot. It can't do everything. But does it do enough? Clearly, it fulfils Harari's criteria for social change as it is a coherent narrative about how the future can be better. But evidence on the ground in 2020 suggests it is broken and inadequate. Perhaps the metaphor of the machine doesn't work either.

To find a starting point for the idea of an economy which resonates more profoundly let's go further back, to before mechanical science, to the archetype of the regenerative process. Here is an alchemical illustration (figure 3 right) which sees that the animation of the earth, its fecundity, is an outcome of a cyclical process: it assumes that the four elements of earth, air, fire and water are animated by the fifth, the life force, the quintessence, represented by the so called 'snake-dragon' that "shall endlessly eat its tail to stay alive". The alchemists believed that the perfection of man and of all things comes through cycles of dissolution and coming together ('solve et coagula') which can be manipulated by those who are chosen and recognise the right time and place ('system conditions'!). They must sacrifice much to achieve this Pearl of Great Price. The process was called the Great Work. Between the advent of the Gutenberg printing press (mid-15th century) and the late 18th century over 4600 titles on alchemy were produced.

Figure 3: "The snake-dragon shall endlessly eat its tail to stay alive"

Credit: British Library

Almost like discussing economics, alchemy was highly symbolic and deemed practical only for the adept, but it represented a story that was at least reaching to grasp the whole; to imagine the whole system at work. It was a lie, yet the alchemists pointed to a truth that we can intuitively recognise: the cycles of earth and life.

In our imaginary, a series of seven insights or episodes moves us from the alchemists pre-science circularity archetype, via its curious diminution in today's economic story, to the structures and processes of real world regenerative systems – revealed thanks to the insights from contemporary science and from complex living systems in particular.

This is about re-contextualising the economy in a contemporary way. To do this, it's important to abandon the simple 'pipework', the engineering image. The economy needs to be contextualised-porous to its environments, and to be working as 'nested' systems. Then it becomes more about aspects of the science of complexity, about scale and the dynamic movement and exchange of nutrients in effective systems. If a body has a metabolism that, via its blood circulation, transforms energy and food materials into nutrients and structures for all of the body, then this is surely about a *metabolistic* approach, set within a nourishing ecosystem. The economy is surely embedded and exchange and circularity intertwined.

For 21st century pioneers Nic Hanauer and Eric Lui[3], an economy looks more like a garden than a mechanism – yes, it's the usefulness of metaphor once more. The original economists, the French physiocrats were also fond of metaphors around the 'natural order' with agriculture as the source of wealth. Interestingly, they also had a deep respect for the Chinese tradition of *wu wei*, which is to set the system conditions to allow 'reigning without ruling'. There are deep roots to our thinking, and many byways: *wu wei* became translated as 'laissez faire' – not quite the same meaning.

Figure 4: Symbol of wu wei

So we are trying to visualise the economy differently as a way of changing perceptions. Curiously, in this imaginary, money *as credit* becomes alchemaical, part of the transformation, it becomes a quintessence, a fifth element, a catalyst.

In alchemy the main reaction took place in one vessel and a process of building order and destroying it, through dissolving and recombining, led to a powder which perfects the imperfect. In a new kind of economics we might settle for some basic heuristic which makes the circularity improve the wellbeing of all that participate and is, indeed, regenerative of the system as a whole.

Playfully in this imaginary, the economy is also treated as being one dynamic process but in order to grasp its essential relationships this process needs to be subdivided.

We therefore move on to discuss the two main cycles of the economy – firstly, the familiar *materials* stocks and flows *(with energy throughput)* and with the actors being producers (firms) and consumers (households). Associated with this materials cycle are four main principles of the circular industrial economy – the 'how to?' of an economy of production and consumption which works long term through circulation. Additional actors can be governments and importers and exporters. These main positions are on the Samuelson economy diagram (figure 2 page 10) as this is a diagram – limited in scope we know – about a production and consumption economy.

Then we look at the second companion cycle concerning access to *money as credit* and *access to the commons* (the commons are the endowed resource base at any one time). Linked to this cycle are two main actors: the creators of money (finance and government); and the owners or guardians of property (land or other scarce assets, like intellectual property). This gives a composite diagram usually associated with Michael Hudson and Dirk Bezemer – of whom, more later. For this monetary cycle we then suggest four associated monetary principles that shape these stocks and flows and point towards more circulation and the creation of more real wealth for all.

This gives a kind of symmetry. The earth, as the vessel of the alchemist, with a *metabolistic* basis – feedback-rich; two cycles, monetary and material with energy as a throughput; and four core principles for each of the two cycles to maintain circulation and increase capitals, 'the commonwealth'.

Economy = one dynamic process, two cycles, four principles of change for each

Hence: Economy = 1 x 2 x 4/4

We move on to start to imagine how the emerging digital revolution might shape the economies of the future. Then, in the seventh and final episode of the imaginary, we distill the elements to start to visualise and imagine a regenerative circular economy. In Kate Raworth's words, this economy needs to be "regenerative and distributive by design."

If it was a checklist then the aspiration for the economy will be:

✓ it works (check);
✓ it's by intention (check);
✓ and it works for all (check).

At the end of this rainbow there is a pot of gold – and the purpose of this adventure only makes sense when it is seen as a system (not as a list) and when its values are exposed. It is aimed at creating for our times a more democratic, a more participatory, system which improves the quality of human life and that which enfolds it. It is supportive of production and consumption but also use and caring, since caring is mostly about natural, social, human and financial capitals (all of them). We declare these as important values: that the future is worth something (inter-generational justice) and that we can and do participate as citizens, *and* producers *and* consumers and have agency there.

Maybe the rainbow never really reaches the ground, it is a perceptual illusion but symbolically it acts like a utopia. And we will always need utopias:

"Utopia lies at the horizon. When I draw nearer by two steps, it retreats two steps. If I proceed ten steps forward, it swiftly slips ten steps ahead. No matter how far I go, I can never reach it. What, then, is the purpose of utopia? It is to cause us to advance."

Fernando Birri, *Argentinian filmmaker*

Through the following seven episodes the imaginary uncovers a Worldview; then Economies are revealed; then Economies are changed and our ideas about them too. It is one process of unfoldment and enfoldment. It's never ending, it's a dynamic not a destination.

0) Worldview pre-science – Circularity as an Archetype

The alchemical illustration (figure 3, page 11) assumed that the four 'known' elements of earth, air, fire and water are animated by the fifth, the life force, the quintessence represented by the snake-dragon. It symbolises the sense of constant re-creation, the infinite cycle of nature's creation and destruction, life and death. The pre-science of alchemy is based on the idea of transformation through iteration, of the person moving towards spiritual perfection, and the truth of the process is revealed through the transmutation of metals. This notion is ages old, being found among the Arabs, the Greeks and before them in ancient Egypt and China.

For many, the idea of making gold from lead, by bringing forth an elixir of transformation from the prima materia *was* the purpose and not a tool for a greater purpose. Something like this narrowness exists today about the economy. Outwardly, the economy is about exchange, about barter between producers and consumers which is represented and facilitated by money that acts like oil in a machine. Money is seen as a medium of *exchange* and a temporary store of value – savings – which allows further investment in production. Money is just seen as a means, a way of getting around barter, not an end.

Figure 5 (below): An alchemist with his family, working a bellows at his furnace. (shows a redistillation flask – the pelican – to right of the furnace). Engraving by J.C. Bentley after A. van Ostade, 1661

Credit: Wellcome Foundation

Just as the alchemical fashion was fading before the Enlightenment's encroachment in the 18th century, Adam Smith talked about the 'great circulation' as through production and exchange came the means to increase the wealth of the economy and improve everyone's position. Smith wanted these exchanges to be free from the landlord, the owner of land or other resource, who might charge a rent for access, an unearned income. Instead he argued that the market should resolve its value in use not in

existence. Making the case for free and fair-to-all competition echoed Aristotle who said "on the whole, you find wealth much more in use than in ownership".

And so the archetype of the economy is and was of *circulation* and of those tools and ideas which promote exchange and a bias against those which inhibit or prevent circulation. The pre-scientific circularity archetype (page 11) can, in this imaginary, prompt a couple of other ideas before it is laid to one side.

Firstly, keeping the alchemical vessel in mind (the *pelican* in figure 5, left), imagine the economy is one process with different faces – it is physical, it is energetic. And it is also informatic (it is about information, form, being shaped).   The process is moved by energy, just as the constant gentle fire below the alchemists' vessel. Secondly, there is an exchange between different material elements in the one process of the economy which, after many cycles, working through *an animating fifth element*, gives the potential of the changed form of a regenerative economic system. Remember, like the production of alchemical gold, an economy is a means not an end.

But if energy and materials, money and the commons (the endowment of resources, including land) are collectively the *imagined* four elements of our new understanding of the economy then there is no quintessence. The fifth element is missing. Kenneth Boulding reminds us that an economy is made up "knowledge, materials and energy"[4]. Unsurprisingly, knowledge, since it 'in-*forms*' or gives meaning and structure to matter, is the missing fifth element. Although conventionally the codeword for this knowledge is 'technology' there is also something important about money if we can stop thinking about it as a commodity that just serves simply as a way of getting around barter. It could be argued that money in a certain role also animates the system, it 'makes the world go round'. It is alive. Since money as credit can be created, for free out of nothing, it's not a fixed commodity, it's not a given. Instead, it's a kind of knowledge, a promise to pay; a 'social construct'. As Ann Pettifor[5] names it, money is an agreement, with a purpose – a share in a better life. Like the snake-dragon, it's the quintessence, it's active and activating. Money is more like rocket fuel than engine oil, to make the mechanical analogy. Most don't even see this. The *potential* for a *regenerative* economy can never be discussed usefully by staying solely with materials, energy and the commons (endowment). We also need to discuss knowledge: technology *and* credit money.

Yet today it seems we can only imagine an economy which is a diminished version of what even the pre-science archetype represented as a regenerative system.

To begin with, it seems many argue that God is dead and the world is dead matter to be operated on. With access to fossil fuel energy we humans are in charge of Life and energy. The economy, including people, reduces to commodities and exchange. Technology is key, technology is the answer they say (but what was the question?!). Growth is the purpose and cure for almost any ill. And what a sleigh ride that has been. Talk about illusions yet calling them real: alchemy was a dead end but today apparently we are to accept instead a constant 'circular' flow of *income and expenditure* around production and consumption; assuming a never ending fossil fuel energy supply; assuming sufficient materials and assuming money is dead, that it's just a commodity and acts simply as a way of getting around barter ('veil over barter').

The economy today is seen a machine for processing resources, a throughput and engineered device made whole by assuming that enclosing and then converting *natural capital* (resources and energy stocks), *social capital* and *human capital* into *financial capital*, solves the problem of closing the loop - since here it is assumed that financial capital is seen to stand for all capitals, for the potential to do anything, and that it can substitute one kind of capital for another - if the price is right. Hubris.

Even in this instrumental version of the linear through-put economy, some sort of circularity of income and expenditure is still assumed to be important But it all looks and feels like a pipe-work analogy, with money standing in for values – since it seems as if everything has its price, and is included in the price. Beyond that, there is an illusion too of precision and control over the system through the automatic mechanism of the market with a few adjustments for 'market failure'.

But since most real world systems are not based on engineer-ing pipework here we put the case that a new starting point for the economy is needed.... a starting point where the general insight recognises that circularity, interdependence and stock maintenance is key in all capitals (because they are not perfectly substitutable). Here we propose that the purpose of the economy needs to be an enduring dynamic set of relationships 'in service to Life' (a phrase from *A Finer Future*[6]. That's a choice, that's strange; it sounds like an economy has a reason outside of itself. Maybe it does and perhaps it always has done.

1) Economy as one dynamic process – comparing circulation in Blood and Money

If a linear, mechanistic analogy for the economy doesn't suffi-ciently capture a way of thinking about real world systems, then what about something more *non-linear* and adaptive? Something where the boundaries are broader and more able to exist long term – something where there is systemic or indirect causation...

The words are a problem in themselves. Everyone gets the idea of direct causation – pull the handle get the result; everyone sees machines connecting input and output. I kick the ball harder and it goes further – it's sort of proportional to effort. Do more, get more. It's a linear relationship. But if output and input are no longer

Figure 6: The Roman god Janus

related in the obvious way then it is non-linear, more dependent on what else is connected within the system. Perhaps we need to go a bit *metabolistic* like an organism or even an organism in context – its ecosystem.

If not machines as a metaphor then... what? These living systems are not just complicated, like a car or aircraft but they are complex and diverse. This means they are dynamic and full of feedback, not just internally but from outside. These living systems can change, we know as we are humans and so we are sensitive to how they are connected and to starting conditions – understanding how I am today also means understanding how I grew up – these systems have histories. They are not pre-determined, or machine-like but neither are they random and disordered, evidently. They can survive and thrive. We are asking if there are *patterns and rules* about these complex, feedback-rich and diverse living systems which help us to think differently, about the economy for example.

What, if anything, is the commonality when it comes to different versions of complex systems such as living organisms – perhaps ecosystems, maybe even cities? Maybe economies....?

The science of these systems is well advanced but the insights and their application in common discourse much less so[7]. To help this along, here we have chosen to visualise two complex systems with circulation – blood and money. Let's consider whether there are some common characteristics between blood and money systems. For a very long time money in an economy has been described as if it were blood in a living creature – blood has to reach every cell for the body to survive healthily yet it flows through large, medium and small channels. Blood is an effective system, it's self-maintaining but the boundary is not just the obvious pipe-work (arteries, veins). It also includes thousands of kilometres of blood capillaries, just wide enough for blood cells to flow through. All the cells of the body's skin are another boundary and then the body is connected to sources of input (e.g. food) and destinations for waste – in a system where this waste is also food for the bigger system beyond the body – the ecosystem. The blood system is nested within other systems.

So the first insight about complex living systems is that they are Janus-faced. Named after the Roman god of "beginnings, gates, transitions, time, duality, doorways, passages, and endings." Janus faced the past and the future and also let's imagine he viewed the smaller and the larger system simultaneously. Arthur Koestler used this idea in his book *Janus: A summing up*[8], one of the first broad based books linking complexity with philosophy. For him, this way of organising was a *holarchy* - nested systems where whole and part have a mutual relationship.

Figure 7: Blood flow through capillary beds

Illustration: Graham Pritchard

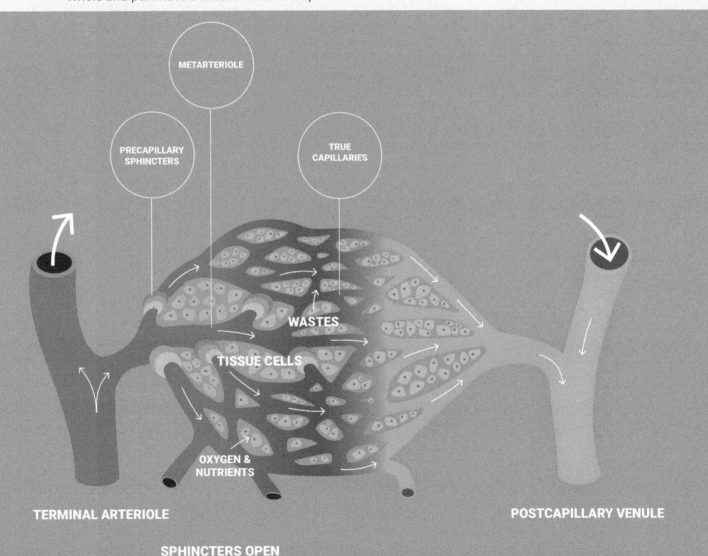

The money circuit of an economy needs to work like the blood system of a body – to be *effective*, it needs to reach the periphery in a nourishing way and everywhere. An effective system is more than an *efficient* one because effectiveness means talking about the whole system and its purpose. Efficiency just means a relationship between input and output, it has no purpose in a systems' sense. As we discuss below, the emphasis in simplified descriptions is usually on efficiency but if we can't see or get a sense of the periphery then we tend to ignore it. Consider the blood flow illustration in figure 7 (page 21). Arguably, *the main action* is at the periphery at the level of the tiny blood capillaries and individual cells. Even this diagram has a misleading sense of the relationships where the temptation is just to notice the big channels (arteries and veins) and the pump (heart) rather than the myriad exchanges where the work is done. In short, it's often tempting to look at *flows* rather than *exchange* functions.

The contemporary world is very focussed on efficiency. This is really a throughput or flow idea, it's about getting more from less. As Walter Stahel has said "the linear economy is driven by the bigger-better-faster-safer syndrome". But this is only part of the picture. In a linear economy, or an economy of machine-thinking, the parts are the focus and whether or not they work well. Working well can mean looking at specific performance targets for example or how inputs are related to outputs. The whole is just the sum of the parts.

But in complex systems, like the ones we are examining here – blood and money – the emphasis is on the relationships, the holarchy (rather than the parts) and on the idea of *effectiveness*. Effectiveness, someone remarked "is efficiency plus *redundancy* over time". In an airplane there are redundant systems, which cover for failure and keep the plane in the air. No one would complain about this as inefficiency – having equipment which is almost never used. In the blood circulation, damage to parts of the system, say bruising or bleeding is not usually fatal. Blood flow is flexible, the body can heal, there is spare capacity for coping. Capillaries can be shut off, blood rerouted. There is redundancy in the blood system, a resilience brought about via the many small pathways, nodes and ability to self-repair, whereas if an efficient 'big flow' pipe in a very efficient system fails then it is often fatal - there is no way back.

Efficiency can mean brittleness. *And effective systems, unlike efficient systems, reveal an interplay between large and small, between flow (delivering/recovering) and exchange, between the system and its environment.* This is why anyone who only wants to talk about efficiency is missing what makes such a system work; they are assuming the contexts. This can be a fatal one-sidedness. Here's a test of it: "it's a great business idea now try and run it in Somalia" (or another failed state). Not impossible but... assuming a benign business context is dumb if we know that all systems are nested. There are subsystems and there are systems which enfold our system. As Michael Braungart, one of the pioneers of cradle to cradle design, notes "we always talk about the forest as well as the trees". Even then, it's another choice of a boundary. In a way,

Figure 8: 'The Window of Vitality': why the health of a system needs a balance of efficiency and resilience

Adapted from: Sally Goerner, Bernard Lietaer and Bob Ulanowicz[9]

Illustration: Graham Pritchard

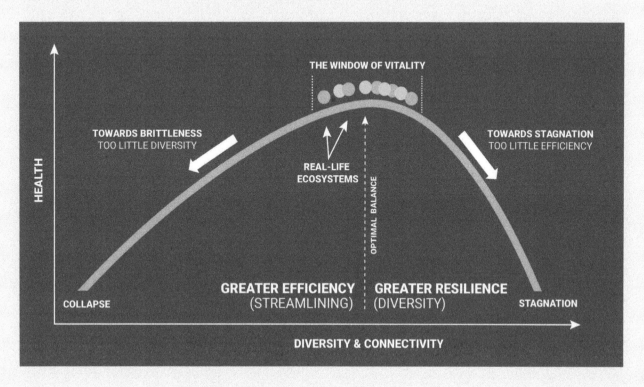

it's odd that he even has to make that point since the trees, the shrubs and other plant and animal life are obviously nested within a forest ecosystem. But he does because it tends to be ignored. He uses the idea, popularised by Peter Drucker, the management science pioneer, that there is a difference between "doing the right thing and doing things right". The former suggests understanding effectiveness and the latter just efficiency – important as it is.

Sally Goerner and Bernard Lietaer helped illustrate what makes an effective system in this graphic (figure 8 below), which could be related to blood, or oxygen or money or energy systems. The outcome for an enduring but adaptable effective system is this interplay between efficiency and resilience. Effectiveness is a system design, or intention, in the real world of change and complex systems. Go too much one way towards efficiency and brittleness follows, go too far the other way towards resilience and then change is very difficult, the system becomes sclerotic and fails.

Another important characteristic of complex living systems is that over time these dynamic systems grow, develop, break down and reorder with strong recognisable patterns too. It looks like this according to Buzz Holling the Canadian ecologist[11]. It's something he calls 'panarchy'. The essential focus of panarchy is to rationalize the interplay in systems between change and persistence, between the predictable and unpredictable. This time the invocation is of the Greek god of nature Pan whose persona also gave an image of unpredictable change... so dynamic living systems are also Pan-like.

Panarchy theory helps us understand how complex systems of all kinds, including ecological, social and economic systems, evolve and adapt. Thomas Homer-Dixon[10] has observed how it shares similarities with other theories about adaptation and change in complex dynamic systems. Its core idea – that systems naturally grow, become more brittle, collapse, and then renew themselves in an endless cycle – recurs repeatedly in literature, philosophy, religion, and studies of human history, as well as in the natural and social sciences. But Buzz Holling has done much more than just

Figure 9 (left): The Greek god Pan. Here he appears as a beautiful youth whose tousled hair and dreamy expression are the only indications that he is an unpredictable woodland being

Credit: The Met

**PANARCHY AND ADAPTIVE CYCLES -
COMPLEX SYSTEMS NATURALLY GROW,
BECOME MORE BRITTLE, COLLAPSE,
AND THEN RENEW THEMSELVES IN AN
ENDLESS CYCLE**

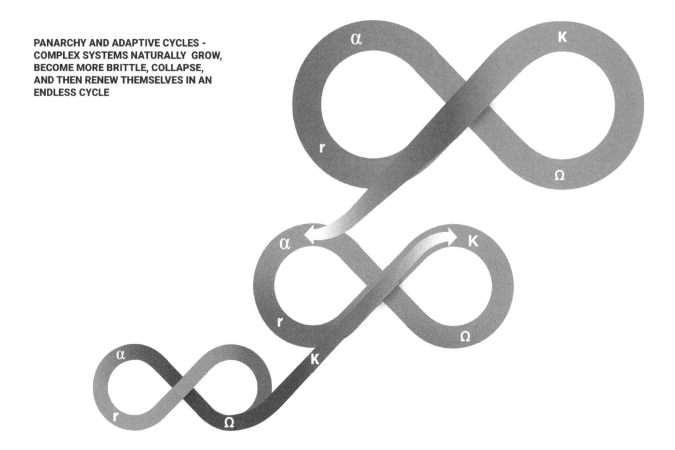

REORGANISATION PHASE
A time of innovation,
restructuring and greatest
uncertainty but with
high resilience.

GROWTH PHASE
Is characterised by: rapid
accumulation of resources
(capitals), competition, seizing
of opportunities, rising level of
diversity and connections, and
high but decreasing, reslience.

CONSERVATION PHASE
Growth slows down as resources
are stored and used largely for
system maintenance. This phase
is characterised by: stability,
certainty, reduced flexibility,
and low resilience.

CREATIVE DESTRUCTION PHASE
This phase is characterised by
chaotic collapse and release of
accumulated capital. This is a
time of uncertainty when
resilience is low but increasing.

restate this old idea. Through his impressive theoretical research since the 1970s, he has made it far more precise, powerful, and useful by distinguishing between potential, connectivity, and resilience; by identifying variations in the system's pace of change as it moves dynamically through its cycle; and by describing the roles of adjacent cycles in the grand hierarchy of cycles..

It does seem that being open to the existence, or rather reality, of interdependent non-linear systems brings us to such a different perspective.

Be it a healthy blood system, body, ecosystem, or money system, in a wider circular economy it appears that a kind of 'circularity' prevails, with adaptive cycles and feedback creating a dynamic stability in the real world systems we see. But they are open systems for all that, powered by a surplus which is the energy from the sun and, to some extent, from the still hot core of the earth.

It's important to note that these dynamic systems are set within the 2nd Law of Thermodynamics which states that order in a system overall declines over time. Coherence, the continual rebuilding of order, depends upon the constant reinjection of surplus energy into the system – think here, for example, of how the process of photosynthesis in a plant leaf uses sunlight each day to build sugars for the plant. Anyone who doesn't integrate energy into their 'economics production function' (their description of what brings about production) is in a world unconnected to our own[12].

Effective, and thus purpose-orientated systems, are character-ised by a constant interplay of efficiency and resilience – around the twin functions we have described of 'flow' and 'exchange'. Such systems, which are Janus-faced or holarchic (nested), are also swept by the interplay of 'remember' and 'revolt', a panar-chy which is both creative and destructive by turns and always changing.

Figure 10 (left): Panarchy Adapted from: Buzz Holling[11].

Illustration: Graham Pritchard

Every economy is a monetary economy as well as a materials, products and services economy. Just as technology is the application of knowledge (as in the popular idea of machinery) so is the creation and use of money as credit. It can act as a stimulus, it's active, more like rocket fuel than the engine oil conceived of in earlier characterisations of the economy. It is deeply intertwined with the role of energy surplus as the means of creating economic growth.

2) Circularity in the Materials Economy – Four principles

"If the society toward which we are developing is not to be a nightmare of exhaustion, we must use the interlude of the present era to develop a new technology which is based on a circular flow of materials such that the only sources of man's provisions will be his own waste products".

Kenneth Boulding, *Economics as a Science*[13]

The everyday textbook economy is an economy of production, consumption and exchange. It is barter with a 'veil of money' over the top so it's about products, components and materials. We know this is primitive but we'll let this go for now. In energy terms, it is powered by fossil fuels today but the shift to renewable energy is crucial and overdue, although maybe not sufficient - so rethinking production and exchange and rebuilding eroded natural capital might give some more space and time for the energetic shift.

In the 1990s, books like the *Ecology of Commerce* by Paul Hawken[14], *Regenerative Design* by Jon T Lyle[15], and *Upsizing* by Gunter Pauli[16] all made the case for a thoroughly modern economy but with more sophisticated materials flows and better product, service and system design. Perhaps Natural Capitalism, published in 1999[17], was the most comprehensive with its focus on natural capital stocks, flows and feedback improvement:

"While industrial systems have reached pinnacles of success, able to muster and accumulate human-made capital on vast levels, natural capital, on which civilization depends to create economic prosperity, is rapidly declining, and the rate of loss is increasing proportionate to gains in material well-being. Natural capital includes all the familiar resources used by humankind: water, minerals, oil, trees, fish, soil, air, etc. But it also encompasses living systems which include grasslands, savannas, wetlands, estuaries, oceans, coral reefs, riparian corridors, tundras, and rainforests."

In *Natural Capitalism*, the authors, Amory and Hunter Lovins and Paul Hawken talked about the four shifts which are needed in the economy. They remain essential today. The four principles are:

1. Rebuild natural capital
2. Radical resource efficiency
3. A shift from goods to services
4. Be bio-mimetic so that waste = food

More on this in a moment. Around this time Bill McDonough and Michael Braungart were writing *Cradle to Cradle: Remaking the Way We Make Things*[18] and for them the three main principles are:

• Celebrate diversity
• Shift to renewables/clean energy
• Waste = food

We have reordered these three McDonough and Braungart principles so as to start with diversity as the pointer towards systems thinking, followed by the energy transformation and finally the materials question, where the important principle is 'waste = food'. The energy shift is discussed briefly in the last episode of the imaginary as is the role of complex adaptive systems where 'diversity is strength' (resilience) but also a source of creativity.

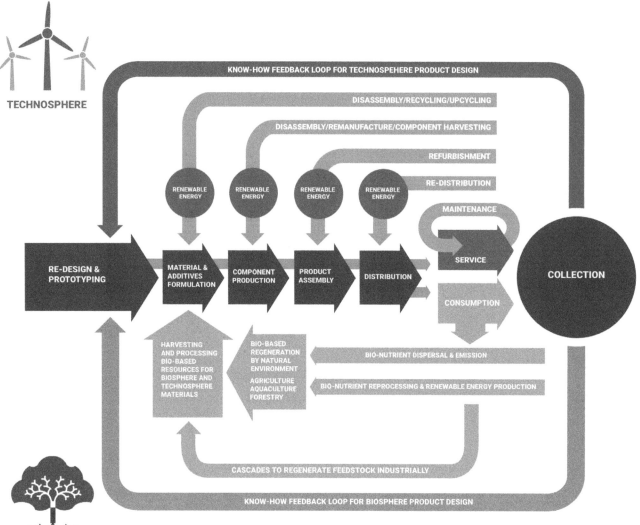

TECHNOSPHERE

KNOW-HOW FEEDBACK LOOP FOR TECHNOSPEHERE PRODUCT DESIGN

DISASSEMBLY/RECYCLING/UPCYCLING

DISASSEMBLY/REMANUFACTURE/COMPONENT HARVESTING

REFURBISHMENT

RE-DISTRIBUTION

RENEWABLE ENERGY

MAINTENANCE

RE-DESIGN & PROTOTYPING

MATERIAL & ADDITIVES FORMULATION

COMPONENT PRODUCTION

PRODUCT ASSEMBLY

DISTRIBUTION

SERVICE

CONSUMPTION

COLLECTION

HARVESTING AND PROCESSING BIO-BASED RESOURCES FOR BIOSPHERE AND TECHNOSPHERE MATERIALS

BIO-BASED REGENERATION BY NATURAL ENVIRONMENT

AGRICULTURE AQUACULTURE FORESTRY

BIO-NUTRIENT DISPERSAL & EMISSION

BIO-NUTRIENT REPROCESSING & RENEWABLE ENERGY PRODUCTION

CASCADES TO REGENERATE FEEDSTOCK INDUSTRIALLY

KNOW-HOW FEEDBACK LOOP FOR BIOSPHERE PRODUCT DESIGN

BIOSPHERE

Figure 11: An iteration of a circular economy showing the two material metabolisms – with a shift to renewables, radical resource efficiency and a shift from goods to services Adapted from: EPEA/Returnity

Illustration: Graham Pritchard

The rebuilding of natural capital is implied in their 'waste = food' principle on the basis that surplus energy is converted through biological processes. Biomimetic design is when we mimic biological and ecological systems, structures and processes in the design of our human-made systems. Like a forest, we need to design in the waste = food principle into our systems: the 'forest feeds the trees'. The forest, with its living soils, and fallen and living plant matter, is a rich stock as well as a source of nutritious flows for all parts of the forest ecosystem. As Bill McDonough says "everything is a resource for something else. In nature, the 'waste' of one system becomes food for another." He'd argue that in the design process there is a need for materials to flow cleanly and safely, uncontaminated with toxic chemicals[19], so that the materials can become 'food' for the circular economy. But we need to go further.

Mcdonough and Braungart also spilt up materials into two circular 'nutrient' flows – those which flow via the biosphere and those which humans use and curate in a 'technosphere'. But the basic stories of *Natural Capitalism* and *Cradle to Cradle* interweave nicely. Another way to look at the different 'nutrient' flows is to ask "where is order rebuilt?" If only humans can restore the order it is a technical nutrient and needs to be kept out of the biosphere if at all possible.

The picture is reasonably plain: think capitals first, the stocks of natural capital are vital, particularly if materials and energy are the foci of discussion. Then visualise the two materials flows, or 'metabolisms', in a circular economy – those which are nutrients for the biosphere and those which are nutrients for the 'technosphere'. In the biosphere are products of consumption (use up/disorder/then regenerate) and in the technosphere primarily products of service (use but do not use up/then restore) respectively. This means that in a circular economy both regenerative and restorative approaches are required to rebuild natural and manufactured capital. Figure 11, an early iteration of the circular economy, is based on the Cradle to Cradle design protocol; it shows the two circular material flows and is often summed up as being 'regenerative and restorative by intention and design'.

The authors of these two books are variously designers, chemists, ecologists and energy efficiency experts and had made inroads into manufacturing, utility businesses, product and service design and more. But the focus was set within the conventional economic perspective. It was 'eco-modern' not 'eco-different'. Since 2010 this work around the circular economy has been strengthened, in the West: after the financial crash of 2008; by the volatility of resource supply, and prices; through growing demand; and the potential offered within a burgeoning digital era. Organisations such as the Ellen MacArthur Foundation[20] have investigated and shaped a vital and bigger picture sense of the business and conventional economic case for a circular economy while keeping some form of 'systems' perspective and showing the overlaps in this modern narrative.

To many, a circular materials economy is inevitable, as the aspirations for several billion new world citizens cannot be met without it; the current resources overshoot may already be disastrous and would be accelerated without the shift to a circular economy. The challenges are enormous, not just from the materials and energy perspective but also from the systems perspective.

McDonough and Braungart asked that we collectively 'celebrate diversity', Lovins that we do 'whole system design'[21] yet their advice is widely ignored or misunderstood. This might simply be because their recommendations are way outside the boundaries we are used to. Coded within 'celebrate diversity' is a way of asking what makes effective, adaptable systems, ones that work on all scales, rather than just efficient large-scale ones – that sort of thinking is way outside most current comfort zones.

Much of the current discussion on the circular economy is attuned to radical energy and materials efficiency in production at large scales. This radical resource efficiency principle is important but it lacks a way of integrating systems requirements such as: the need to be regenerative; the need to address 'stock maintenance' concepts rather than just 'flows'; and the need to consider system structures that are a combination of efficient flow channels at the large-scale and effective exchange at the small or medium scale.

And since an economy is not a pipework but more like a complex and dynamic ecosystem or biological system (e.g. blood, as described earlier) there are also unexamined and possibly incorrect assumptions in many of the current circular economy storylines.

Incorrect assumption 1: production efficiency leads, it's a kind of 'digital techno-economic worldview'. In nine out of ten storylines it's assumed a big picture circular Economy is firstly about a supply side, production-orientated approach and that demand is assumed to arise in equal force; so that whatever is created will be bought, at a price (Say's Law[22]).

Incorrect assumption 2: no role for managing demand. Here, it's wrongly assumed that overall demand management, and money, debt and banks have no long-term active role in the economy.

Incorrect assumption 3: it's about incentivising the direction of material flows, not linear but circular flows – and capitals come second. This is all about assuming that materials circulation is the only thing – here it's the blind spot about *capitals* again. In most current circular economy storylines critical questions are ignored.

Natural capital, financial capital, who owns it and who determines access to it? Can we ask about the balance between extraction and retention of value and the circulation of value throughout the system as a result of using some of the capitals?

From the above, there is a suspicion, perhaps a certainty, that in reality a naive circular economy of products, components and materials is in an intimate dance with natural and financial capital. And that this has much more to do with the ownership of assets and the economic rents (unearned income) paid to access those assets rather than the nuts, bolts and ploughshares of actual production and consumption, and the circulation of value throughout the economic system.

It seems some of our regenerative circular economy is MIA (Missing In Action!). It's time to find it, if indeed that is the case, but before we do, here is an attempt to update the principles of the circular economy with four rules for the productive materials cycle:

01 RULE ONE
Regenerate and restore capitals including natural and social capital

02 RULE TWO
Be biomimetic ('waste = food' and 'diversity=strength')

03 RULE THREE
Shift from selling goods to selling services or performance

04 RULE FOUR
Optimise the whole system (be effective not just resource efficient)

3) Circularity in the Monetary Economy – the role of money as credit and access to the commons

Rather obvious as it may seem, here's a reminder that the Economy (big E) is both monetary and energetic. To obtain economic growth requires not just creating and using an energy surplus but - alongside a physical environment which is suitable for human and other life - economic growth also needs that happy human invention called money and credit. That sufficient money is required as a medium of exchange is fairly obvious but to bring

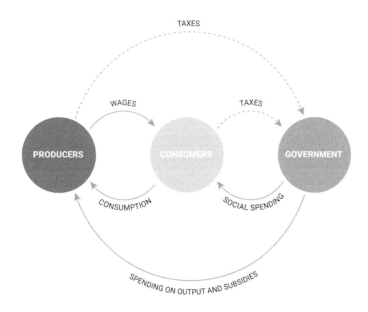

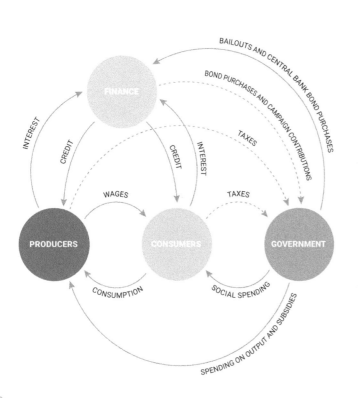

forward production, beyond investing any funds already saved, requires credit made available as a loan, or money created as 'additional spending power' without interest. Economic growth then means the debt can be repaid or, at least, the interest payments on the loan can be supported without eating into the economy. So far, so normal except that this approach begins to reveal additional and vital active nodes in the economy which sit alongside firms (producers), households (consumers) and government.

It's time to get better acquainted with Michael Hudson and Dirk Bezemer. These economists are authors of a very powerful article *Finance is Not the Economy*[23] which is the source of the information in the second (bottom left) and third (over page) diagrams.

Here is the pipework (top left) we know well enough – there is no trade sector for simplicity.

In their language, one active node in the monetary economy is described as Money/Finance and then a related node described as Real Estate/Monopolies which - like some aspects of the banking and finance node - stands for assets which most easily attract economic rents when they are accessed. The crucial difference between earned and unearned income and between profits, wages, interest and rents will become clear.

Here is the Finance node (bottom left)

Here is the Real Estate/Monopolies node – the land and properties or 'enclosed commons' for some commentators. Some of the return for this is based on a charge for scarcity itself: another phrase for economic rent, or unearned surplus. We can see the main players now:

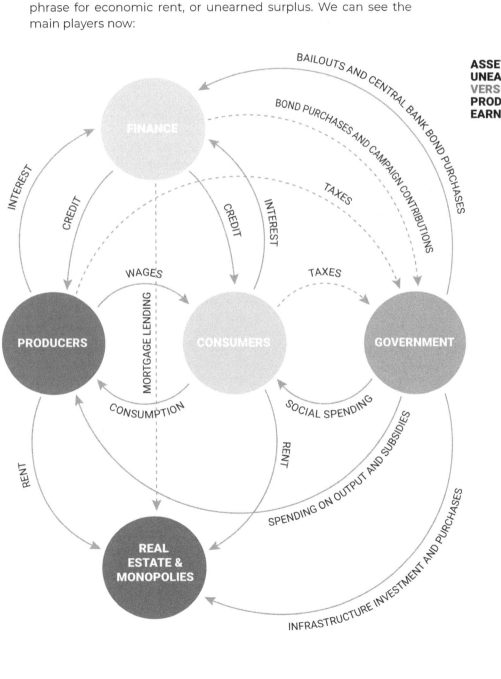

ASSETS AND UNEARNED INCOME
VERSUS
PRODUCTION/CONSUMPTION EARNED INCOME

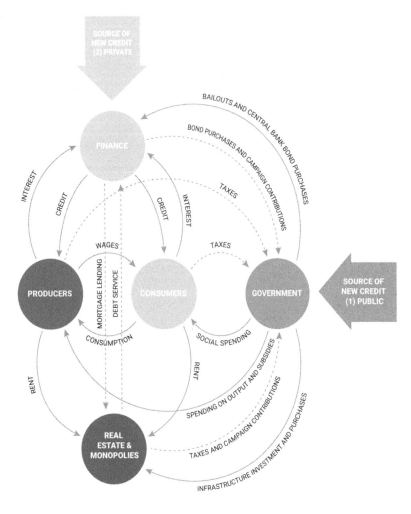

In figure 12 left, the points at which money can be created and applied is also illustrated. The main distinction Hudson and Bezemer wish to illustrate is between economic rents – unearned income - and earned income from production and consumption (from the conversion of materials and energy into new goods and services). The former relates to much of banking and finance (interest as rents - see pg36) and is attached to existing assets, especially copyright (IP) and real estate.

So this is the Economy fully wired, not the very partial, very incomplete image from the Samuelson text book:

In the Money/Finance node (figure 12) it's important to state the obvious: that additional money can be created out of nothing ('ex nihilo') by the virtue of institutions with banking licences making loans and that this is additional spending. Money is not some sort of commodity in fixed supply that is then shuffled around. Since there can be additional money – there are magic money trees(!) – then it is reasonable to ask who is creating it and where does this additional money go?

Figure 12: The economy After Michael Hudson and Dirk Bezemer[23].

Illustration: Graham Pritchard

The answers, for some economists (for example Steve Keen, Stephanie Kelton, and within the group known as the post-Keynesians) is that there are two magic money trees in any economy which controls its own (sovereign) currency- like the USA, UK, Japan or China.

Number one. The government can supply as much money as it requires by spending it into existence[24] and then taxing to ensure stable prices. This is 'our' magic money tree in a democratic society.

The second magic money tree is available to the banking sector as described above (no, they are not just intermediaries and do not require reserves to make loans[2]. Banks make an assessment of the risk involved and the return on a loan likely over time. In practice, this additional money (money as credit) is currently, and overwhelmingly, placed into assets like real estate, shares on the stock exchange, intellectual property, insurance, big data and so on. This allows for both capital value to increase, especially if there is economic growth, and income to be earned by charging for access to the assets. The important thing to recognise about these assets is that they are limited in supply, access can be sold advantageously, part of it is a surplus. This surplus is of course 'rent' of one kind or another, a payment to owners of scarce resources, originally the landlord in the case of land/real estate. The term 'economic rent' is a description of the return more generally which is above that which competition would generate – it's an unearned surplus. Banking, according to Michael Hudson, earns economic rents too. Renting money is called interest.

Although there is an intimate connection between the invention and deployment of money and its use in buying assets and generating economic rent on these assets, it sits alongside the second of the additional nodes in the expanded economy: Real Estate and Monopolies.

So now let's consider figure 12 (illustration). Alongside any discussion on Real Estate and Monopolies we need to discuss the idea of the commons. The human, cultural and physical endowment of the world – its land, atmosphere, oceans, water cycles, mineral deposits, the designs for machinery, accumulated knowledge and social data, products or systems – can all be seen as 'commons', a 'commonwealth' which can be used variously to achieve the outcomes we desire in our societies. In earlier times, managed commons were often the norm in many parts of the world, as Elinor Ostrom has pointed out[25]. And it's important to note here that the important discussion is about access to the commons. Commons were and are not owned by individuals but, instead, accessed and managed most often by the group of people who used/use them. Alternatively, these commons of the world can be seen as having value only when 'enclosed', as private property, and then 'husbanded' correctly for which a suitable compensation is then due to its owner. Nowadays, of course, this is often the dominant perspective on the commons – the ones that remain and have not yet been enclosed!

In classical economics this factor of production, described as 'land,' was distinctive, but in later formulations of economics (the neo-classical) at the end of the 19th century, land had been lumped together with other kinds of capital, principally by US economist John Clark[26] partly in order to defeat the journalist turned politician Henry George. George had powerfully explored the social tension of the late 19th century USA in his hugely popular book *Progress and Poverty*[27] as primarily due to the effects of economic rents payable to the owners of private property. George and his followers were after some of the unearned income as a source of revenue, and relief: especially through a land tax, rather than taxing enterprise or workers.

George failed, although his influence was widespread at the turn of the 20th century and in the politics of the Progressive Era, extending long after his own death in 1897. Labour economist George Soule believed Henry George to be "by far the most famous American economic writer" and "author of a book which probably had a larger world-wide circulation than any other work on economics ever written".

According to Gaffney and Harrison[28], economics in its neo-classical refurbishment meant that land became less visible in the theory while social welfare and economic growth alleviated the condition of the poor. The commons only really began to resurface again during the 1960s especially through the environmental movement. Perhaps it might help to say that recently there has been a growing visibility on who owns land and these other original sources of wealth - the world's endowment of commons[29].

It's clear that a stumbling productive economy with low growth but growing wealth and income inequality, due to the ownership of real estate, intellectual property, financial instruments, stocks and shares, has brought back interest in the difference between 'earned' and 'unearned income'. It seems that inequality generated this way is a feature, not a bug, in the system!

In 2016, Rana Foroohar describes this in her book *Makers and Takers* and, in her critique of unearned income, talks of 'rent seeking' and the 'return of the rentier'[30]. It's very much a live issue. Since we are trying to make sense of real world stocks, flows and feedback we also think, like Hudson and Bezemer, it is helpful to have owners of fixed assets or enclosers of the commons (the resource base) made visible as some of the major actors in the economy.

As a result, the overall Hudson and Bezemer diagram (figure 12) is more complicated but it is worth focussing on the main nodes. We have the physical (materials and energy) economy of production, consumption and exchange on the one side and, on the other, we have the Money/Finance system and Real Estate/ Monopolies which attract returns to the asset owners for allowing access. The illustration show the two aspects of the one economic process.

The basic corrective offered by Michael Hudson and Dirk Bezemer is that money as credit must circulate better in productive and competitive ('free and fair for all') environments. Money as credit should rebuild productive infrastructure (capital) or productive capacity rather than being concentrated in the dead assets cycle (the FIRE economy as Hudson and Bezemer describe it – Finance, Insurance and Real Estate). This assets cycle is where circulation is so much more about inflating asset bubbles than in the world of production and consumption. It also recognises that the demand side of the economy is as important as the supply side - the production side; and that expenditure happens before income.

As a reminder, all this is set within our assumption that real world systems are complex adaptive systems. An enduring and effective, not just short term and efficient, economic system is the aim. It's a heuristic for sure but its main characteristics are around adjusting stocks and flows and feedback in the monetary and physical economy; in some ways it's very simple.

For us, there's a need to restore additional money circulation in the economy by injecting spending into sectors which spend on goods and services rather than those that buy assets which create economic rents ('unearned surplus'). Investment is hugely important so there's also a need to regenerate the shared infrastructure upon which a liveable world, including all markets, is built[31]. At the same time, it's important to shrink the tendency for wealth accumulating assets to be preferred over production and consumption, while at the same time building up the commons and their associated natural and social capital.

Just as we've described some basic principles for a circular materials economy which makes it possible to think of better circulation rather than depletion and waste, then here with the monetary economy it might be possible to describe some principles for better money circulation, rather than extraction and waste. We have chosen just four principles.

4) Four basic principles for the monetary cycle

Principle 1 is: Distribute a Universal Basic Dividend. For decades around the world, the share of wages in the national economies of the developed world has been stagnant or falling and the growth of the 'precariat' (the short term, contract/outsourced or self-employed worker) has expanded hugely. This process is happening even when the impact of Artificial Intelligence and automation has hardly yet been felt and has led to a growing interest in an old idea: some form of basic income. Only it's not an income, since this makes it sound as something earned or given; rather it is a *basic dividend*. In the economy which has both production and

Above: cuckoo chick in redstart nest

consumption but also money and the commons (the resources, or endowment, of the earth) then a basic dividend is just that: a *dividend*, a share of the return from allowing others to use – to 'enclose' in the old term – part of the commons. It is a citizen's share of fees on enclosure. A limited example is the Alaskan Permanent Fund where, in order for business to use some of Alaska's natural resources (in this case oil), fees are paid into a dividend fund which is then distributed to citizens directly.

"In the current COVID -19 crisis many businesses will be saved by injections of capital from the government. There is no reason why one of the conditions of rescue should not be expanded shareholding."

Another approach is to use employee share ownership so that the dividends from enclosure are shared with employees. In the current COVID-19 crisis many businesses will be saved by injections of capital from the government. There is no reason why one of the conditions of rescue should not be expanded shareholding.

The basic dividend, however it is constructed[32], is a key to making sure there is enough demand for the goods and services produced in the economy. Business needs customers and customers need income. Even so, in an era of easy overinvestment and then overproduction[33] and a fragmenting workforce, it's tough going in another direction. But in future we will need customers who can pay their share of the full costs of production which come from redesigning products and services to fit a circular economy. And as the poster slogan proclaims: "a basic dividend is not left or right, it's progress". It's just very practical and it better fits the world we are in. Harking back to the old capital versus labour dichotomy (and assuming full time work) is primitive, it's a gloss on the forces assumed to be at play today. As a long-time advocate, Guy Standing[34] says a basic dividend or income gives numerous advantages. It is worth quoting him at length:

"The main reasons for supporting a basic income, as far as I'm concerned are ethical, not economic. I'm an economist, but I see them as ethical. The first is that a basic income is a matter of social justice. The wealth and income of all of us has far more to do with the efforts of our ancestors and many generations than anything you or I do for ourselves. If we allow private inheritance of wealth and influence and status and so on, we should also have social inheritance. In a sense a basic income would be a sort of social dividend.

Now, it's a very important social dividend because the second and third reasons for supporting a basic income are, first, that it would enhance freedom. If I have basic *income security, I have more freedom. The freedom to say no to an oppressive or abusive relationship or an exploitative employer. The freedom to go forth in society as an equal. That's very important.*

The third reason is that the basic income would give people a sense of basic security. We know from many sources that basic security improves your IQ. It improves your mental stability. It improves your capacity to make long term strategic decisions and to act in a dignified way in which you are giving forth values and attitudes that stem from having security. So people who have security are more altruistic. They're more tolerant of others. They don't support political extremism. They tend to see themselves as citizens. I think that's a very important thing.

Then.... the other reason, as an economist, is at the moment the level of inequality is rising so fast and will not come down through the traditional ways of raising wages. We will not see real wages on average rising much in OECD countries, in Germany, the United States, France, Britain, Japan. They've been stagnating for years and years, and they will continue to stagnate as long as globalization continues and as long as the technological revolution continues and there is a huge overhang of existing debt to be serviced. So we must realize that our income distribution system is collapsing and the basic income would be a way of building a new distribution system. It's not a panacea. It's not by itself. It's one of a number of policies....(an additional factor) is, of course, the robots, the feeling that automation and robots are going to displace millions and millions of people. I think it's disruptive but I think there's going to be plenty of work but that work is not paying good incomes. And a basic income could be seen as a preparation for the disruptive effects of robots and automation.

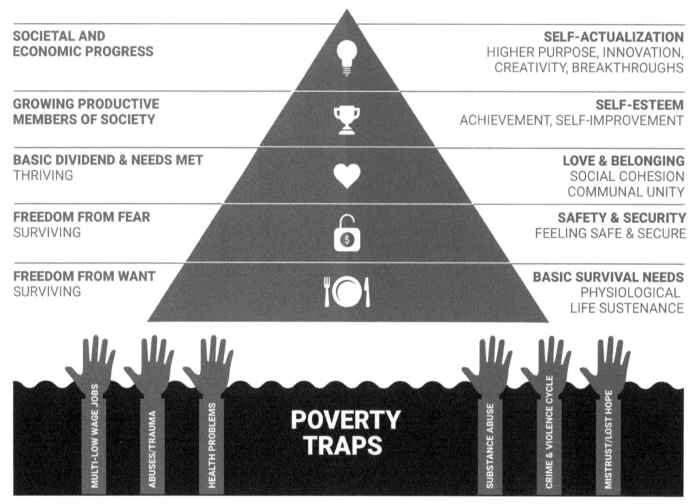

BASIC DIVIDEND EFFECTS

NEEDS

SOCIETAL AND ECONOMIC PROGRESS

SELF-ACTUALIZATION
HIGHER PURPOSE, INNOVATION, CREATIVITY, BREAKTHROUGHS

GROWING PRODUCTIVE MEMBERS OF SOCIETY

SELF-ESTEEM
ACHIEVEMENT, SELF-IMPROVEMENT

BASIC DIVIDEND & NEEDS MET
THRIVING

LOVE & BELONGING
SOCIAL COHESION
COMMUNAL UNITY

FREEDOM FROM FEAR
SURVIVING

SAFETY & SECURITY
FEELING SAFE & SECURE

FREEDOM FROM WANT
SURVIVING

BASIC SURVIVAL NEEDS
PHYSIOLOGICAL
LIFE SUSTENANCE

POVERTY TRAPS

MULTI-LOW WAGE JOBS

ABUSES/TRAUMA

HEALTH PROBLEMS

SUBSTANCE ABUSE

CRIME & VIOLENCE CYCLE

MISTRUST/LOST HOPE

Figure 13 (above): Basic dividend and Maslow's heirarchy of needs

Illustration: Graham Pritchard

*The... final factor ... is what I would call a political imper-
ative. If we do not have a new system that gives people,
ordinary people in the precariat, basic income security,
we're going to see more and more Donald Trumps; and I,
for one, dread that."[34]*

Principle 2 is: 'Tax Shift'. The logic of the tax system will also
need to change. At present, the assumption is that most taxes
need to come from labour – from income – and from consumption, with a decreasing amount from company profits or capital
gains and very little coming from the use of resources. Indeed,
it is notorious that even after 100 years the fossil fuel industry
draws on subsidies either in production or in avoiding a contribution towards the other costs (such as air pollution) caused by
fossil fuel combustion. A long discussion has, over the years, drawn
on switching taxes from renewables, including people (earned
income), to all non-renewables. This might seem like taxes on just
mineral resources but, in fact, it's also aimed at those asset classes
in Hudson and Bezemer's 'monopolies and real estate' category
and would include aspects of intellectual property, financial transactions and capital gains. But such taxes would not be placed on
profits from a productive economy, especially those profits which
were reinvested. The shift is away from upping the costs of the
productive economy and towards discouraging activity where
unearned income or economic rents are visible. It has a strong
environmental rationale too: such a tax shift would promote circulation and continued use of products, components and materials rather than the extraction of new resources. Also, since these
reuse and recovery activities are more labour intensive it can give
another uplift to job opportunities.

A systemic but positive cycle in the economy starts to become
visible. A basic dividend provides security and autonomy, allows
enterprise or small scale working to be viable and also increases
demand for goods and services. A tax shift away from wages and
production profits encourages use of labour, encourages investment and entrepreneurship and simultaneously discourages use
of raw materials and damps down the asset cycle (which lowers

housing costs for example). It would also provide some of the taxation which an appropriate basic dividend deserves. In a way, it's about taking unearned income and giving it as 'unearned income' to everyone while supporting a circular materials economy of 'closing the loop', 'slowing the flow', 'narrowing the resource palette' and stimulating perhaps, the needed investment in infrastructure. The increasingly popular idea of a 'Green New Deal' in many countries[35] meshes here seamlessly. Because money is active and money does grow on trees there are more good things to say about basic dividend, tax shifts and infrastructure spending - such policy developments could help with the shift to a renewables-based energy system and perhaps widespread regenerative agriculture. More about food and farming later.

Principle 3 is: arrange a Debt Jubilee. The two money trees are the government/central bank (if it controls its own currency) and the private banks. Credit can be created and it's a powerful human invention. It's a technology. Who does it and for what reason matters a great deal. It is possible to issue direction as to the criteria for private creation of credit – Richard Werner says that credit guidance has always been in use and is very effective[2] - so that asset bubbles do not remain the most salient feature of economies experience around the world. However, stepping back a little, money is a utility, a tool, so firstly it needs to be a good servant to the economy, not its master and certainly not its religion. The last would be an inversion of all that is good. In many ways the old saying is accurate: the *love* of money is the root of all evil. Not money per se but the desire to accumulate rather than circulate, to put money first, to make it scarce and charge tribute for its use. This debate is rooted, like the enclosure of the commons, in a very long period of history. David Graeber has written a most illuminating book called *Debt: the first 5000 years*[36].

Interestingly, all religions had an injunction against 'usury': making money (as 'interest') on money and many pre-Roman civilisations understood that debt was onerous and arranged periodic debt cancellation ('debt jubilees'). Money is like the endowment of the earth and like all the infrastructure created by past and present generations - a kind of commons or public utility. Perhaps also, as a kind of 'commons', the enclosure of money should be subject to more conditions giving guidance for its issuance. A form of 'debt jubilee' is needed now for quite a simple reason - the debt overhang is so large that it is dampening spending in the productive economy. While an input of cash is linked primarily to reducing indebtedness, since a debt jubilee is universal it means that, for those without debt, it acts as an immediate boost to spending while still being fair to all. There are moral and ethical entanglements throughout economics, and deciding what is fair is just one of them.

If the physical world has to deal with an ongoing and substantial legacy of materials and energy waste and pollution, the monetary economy has to deal with the legacy of 'financial pollution' (as Adair Turner describes debt in *Between Debt and the Devil*[37]), in order to reset and transform the economic system. By arranging a 'quantitative easing for the people' and/or a debt jubilee[38], and by ensuring support for an adequate basic dividend, governance is doing that resetting. To ignore debt would be like ignoring the impacts of the carbon already released into the atmosphere as if they did not affect today and tomorrow.

As the role of governance is properly seen as one of creating the enabling conditions ('rules of the game') for a thriving economy, with much more devolvement of power to local and regional bodies, its responsibility around money is one of the greatest. In the opinion of economist John Kay[39] this is all of a one with a thriving market economy: "almost all the strength of modern market economies is based on directing entrepreneurial activity from rent seeking into wealth creation." Government can use its money creating and directing power to implement principle four of the monetary cycle:

Principle 4 is: build Infrastructure, build the Commons. *The commons* is the wealth that we inherit or create together and must pass on, undiminished or enhanced, to our children. Our collective wealth includes the gifts of nature, civic infrastructure, cultural works and traditions, and knowledge. But it's important to say that the commons are not just a resource. A commons is a resource plus a defined community and the protocols, values and norms devised by the community to manage its resources[40]. Many resources urgently need to be managed as comons, such as the atmosphere, oceans, genetic knowledge and biodiversity. There is no commons without 'commoning' – the social practices and norms for people (the 'commoners') to manage a resource for collective benefit. Forms of commoning naturally vary from one commons to another because humanity itself is so varied. And so there is no 'standard template' for commons; merely shared patterns and principles. The commons must be understood, then, as a verb as much as a noun. A commons must be animated by bottom-up participation, personal responsibility, transparency and self-policing accountability.

One of the great unacknowledged problems of our time is the 'enclosure' of the commons. Enclosure can be seen in the patenting of genes and lifeforms, the use of copyrights to lock up creativity and culture, the privatisation of land and water, and attempts to transform the open Internet into a closed, proprietary marketplace, among many other enclosures. Enclosure privatises and commodifies resources that belong to a community or to everyone, and dismantles a commons-based culture (that's often geared towards co-production and co-governance) with a market order (money-based producer/consumer relationships and hierarchies). Markets often tend to have thin commitments to localities, cultures and ways of life; for any commons, however, these are indispensable.

The classic commons are small-scale and focused on natural resources; an estimated two billion people around the world depend upon commons of forests, grasslands, fisheries, water, wildlife and other natural resources for their everyday subsistence[40]. But the contemporary challenge for such commoners is to find new structures of law, institutional form and social practice that can enable diverse sorts of commons to work at larger scales and to protect their resources from Market or State enclosure. There's an important role here for a new kind of enabler government: to create the enabling conditions that help commoners build these new kinds of commons. Here, enabler government has a key role to play in using its money creating and directing power to help build these commons and commons infrastructures.

The ground breaking work of Michel Bauwens and colleagues in the peer-to-peer and sharing economy movement has shown that new commons forms and practices are needed at all levels – local, regional, national and global – and there is a need for new types of federation among commoners and linkages between different tiers of commons[40].

Building the commons and associated commons infrastructures means enabling or creating resources which are primarily governed by their users - these suit the smaller operations without much capital and are low cost or replicable. Probably both. Examples include platform cooperatives where the commons *is* the software. There are many examples of digital commons, especially around the potential to have a stake in the data to which individuals have contributed. In physical spaces, the whole infrastructure around the likes of maker labs, community land trusts, use of municipal lots, community kitchens etc. can have a very strong sense of being managed by the users not the state. The 'Partner State' is about making opportunities available rather than deciding how the commons are used, and connecting an ecosystem of tools and enterprise to ensure, if possible, the cascading of materials and energy within the very important networks and nodes of these complex commons systems. The role of enabler governance here is to make sure the monetary 'capillary beds' do their job, enhance the exchange function and build value with what the communities of commoners already have.

By addressing these four principles of the monetary circuit, the government can discourage lending into existing assets rather than production and, with the tax shift described, government is able to increase the employability of labour and the conservation of mineral and manufactured 'stocks'. This approach also does a good job of decreasing today's wealth and income inequality which is so much based on owning assets like real estate or shares and on the current creation and rapid flow of money into these assets – in short, asset price inflation which has been a Quantitative Easing policy aim in recent years[41]. Rebuilding natural and social capital rather than just financial capital is the logical outcome of the adjustment to the monetary circuit.

The flurry of ideas here, some of them less well understood by the general public than others, becomes meaningful within the basic notion of adjusting the stocks, flows and feedback of materials, energy and money in favour of an effective, 'circularity'-focussed system across an expanded notion of the 'economy'.

In a transformative circular economy, it is clearly essential to include open discussion on the monetary aspect of the economy including the nodes of Money/Finance and Real Estate/Monopolies, as well as the commons - our collective resource endowment - and how it is controlled or enclosed. In many ways money can even be seen as a 'commons' since it is often thought of as a 'something', a medium of exchange, a unit of measure and store of value provided by government, a resource which is usable by anyone for almost any transaction. Then the whole of the discussion in this section is similar to that around Real Estate/Monopolies: it is about who has access, who creates and who constrains and directs access and at what price. Most money creation is enclosed by private interests these days – at least in normal times. In difficult times, like the 2020 recession, the public money creation takes over and tries to preserve private asset values.

HOUSE PRICE INDICES
EURO AREA AND EU AGGREGATES
INDEX LEVELS (2015=100)

Euro area ▬▬▬   EU ▬▬▬   *Euro QE began Q2 2015

Figure 14: House price indices in the EU and Euro area (Euro Quantitative Easing began in March 2015) Source: Eurostat

Illustration: Graham Pritchard

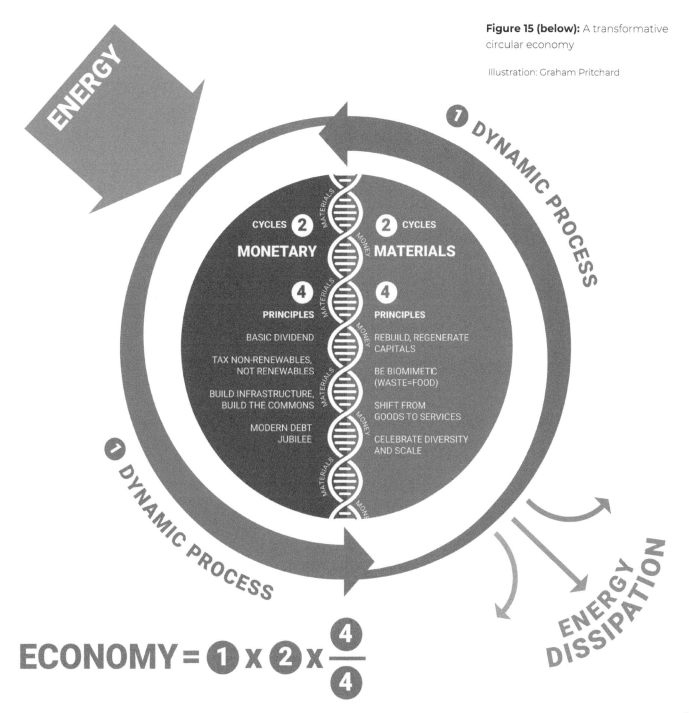

Figure 15 (below): A transformative circular economy

Illustration: Graham Pritchard

ENERGY

① DYNAMIC PROCESS

① DYNAMIC PROCESS

CYCLES ② MONETARY

② CYCLES MATERIALS

④ PRINCIPLES

BASIC DIVIDEND

TAX NON-RENEWABLES, NOT RENEWABLES

BUILD INFRASTRUCTURE, BUILD THE COMMONS

MODERN DEBT JUBILEE

④ PRINCIPLES

REBUILD, REGENERATE CAPITALS

BE BIOMIMETIC (WASTE=FOOD)

SHIFT FROM GOODS TO SERVICES

CELEBRATE DIVERSITY AND SCALE

ENERGY DISSIPATION

$$\text{ECONOMY} = ① \times ② \times \frac{④}{④}$$

Equally important is the dialogue on the physical aspect of the economy, the stocks and flows of materials and energy that take place through the processes of production, consumption and exchange. In these discussions, we also need to factor in the demand side as well as the supply and to distinguish between 'makers' and 'takers'.

Let's return briefly to this equation:

Economy = one dynamic process, two cycles, four principles of change for each

Hence: Economy = 1 x 2 x 4/4. It's one vessel, the earth with a *metabolistic* basis, two cycles (monetary and materials, with energy as a throughput) and with 4 principles for each cycle. The aim is to increase stocks, and effective flows. It's never complete.

In the next episode of the imaginary we go back to system structures, because these systems are not pipe-works but act more like an organism within an ecosystem and this suggests something about how and where value is created and distributed in the economy.

5) Digital Revolution - or the Terrors and Liberation of a digital world

To say that digital changed and is changing the world every bit as profoundly as did the 15th century Gutenberg printing press, the steam engine, the internal combustion engine or electrical energy is no longer to say very much. Like many such changes they are profound because they are usually multifaceted. As Jeremy Rifkin points out, the digital revolution is the coming together of a number of technologies to become a general purpose technology[42]. Just one example that has been documented by Mariana Mazzucato[31]: the smart phone was the 2007 integration of six technologies, most of them, incidentally, developed in the public, rather than the private, realm.

The digital revolution is doing two things simultaneously. On the one hand, it can crash the price of production and distribution by introducing precision automation coupled with artificial intelligence (AI). On the other hand, through the process of disintermediation ('cutting out the middleman'), digital technologies are reducing the traditional connections between the producer of goods and services and the customer or user. A casual examination of what Uber and Didi have done to taxi services or Amazon to retail or Airbnb and Booking.com to accommodation makes the point.

Disintermediation is then replaced by a new intermediation based around the digital platform giants who can get great cost advantage if they get the process to scale. Although some people don't recognise this as only the start of revolutionary change others do. Systems thinker at Santa Fe Institute Brian Arthur,[43] for example, suggests that the age-old 'problem of production is over' and now instead there is a new problem based around the incredible potential for overproduction, proliferation of access over ownership and the on-demand service economy.

For these digital giants, it is really quite hard to make much of a return on the huge investment required without the usual tools of controlling market share, branding, technological/IP propriety, replacing workers with machines and/or casualising the workforce. Being Number 1 is not enough, being the only one is better. But then making gets swamped by taking – production is replaced by rent seeking which, if the overall costs are slashed, might still feel OK for the customers who still have work and some spare money to spend. Yet thoughts will turn to a basic dividend (as discussed earlier).

It's a simplification but large economies of scale deliver excellent digital tools for the global world: standardised; robot-manufactured; sophisticated. Reward includes rents because in many parts of the world the reality is that the digital sector is often a monopoly or is dominated by under a dozen firms.

With systems theory, we can see that such a situation is often based on a simplified, standardised, volume-throughput but it's perhaps a brittle system, albeit one that is able to control some aspects of 'scarcity'. Let's call it the structured 'flow' side of the system. It works well most of the time. Yet for these systems there is always a counterpart. This is not the 'just what's not yet absorbed' part of the economy, something seen as remnant puddles of backwardness and poverty, waiting for their turn. The counterpart, if the analogy of living systems carries some power of explanation, is the part of the system that is networked, complex, *exchange-based*, carries redundancy, and is resilient to shocks. Imagine the apple tree (figure 17).

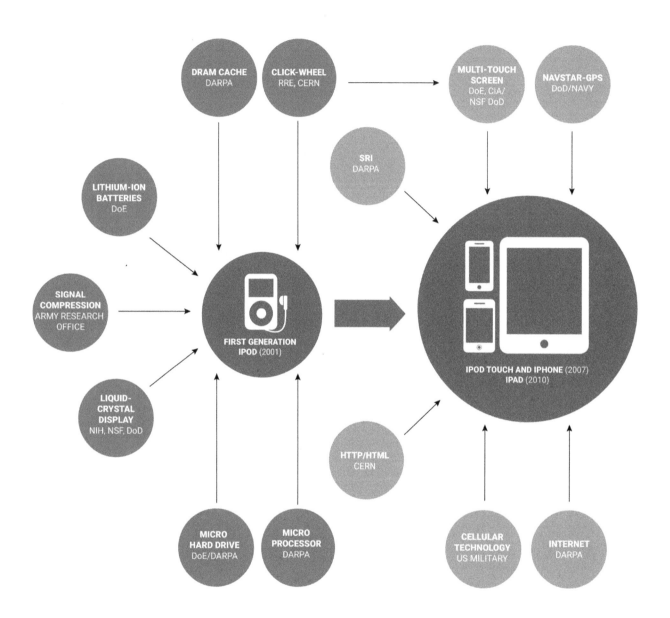

Figure 16: What makes the iPhone so smart?

Adapted from: Mariana Mazzucato[31]

Illustration: Graham Pritchard

Integrated human communities have always had this exchange function or character even if most of the economic activity is non-money. For example, without underplaying the immiseration that can accompany its extremes - living in the barrio or the slum – many low income communities are vibrant places economically. We see this in Kevin McCloud's Mumbai film *Slumming It*[44] and in John Turner's classic work *Housing By People*[45] that documents the creativity of low income communities in the settlements of Peru. And to improve such places does not necessarily mean trying to play the game of efficiency and scale and hoping something good falls out of it. Instead, building the commons, in terms of land, water and sanitation infrastructure security, would be essential as a vital and underpinning first step. It's about building on what is there. Yet as well as such natural resource-based commons, there is also this new commons that is relevant to such communities – information and connectivity.

As many in the more developed world are simultaneously discovering, digital has another, liberating edge to it as well. This new information 'commons' is potentially as powerful as the discovery of the oil reserves of a previous era. Paul Mason[46] talks a lot about how the falling price of digital tools, products and connection can enable what he calls the possibility of 'socially produced goods'. Buy a smart phone and a connection and someone immediately has a business tool of immense flexibility – the DGML approach (design globally, manufacture locally) becomes more the name of the 21st century game around 'celebrating diversity'. The digital links with the important monetary tools of basic dividend, tax shifting and commons-based infrastructure investment are also obvious.

The decline of formal employment and long term careers makes such digital trends ever more attractive as a creative and necessary way out. The existence of 'platform cooperatives' – software which returns the benefits to the users – and cooperatives of all kinds have boomed, alongside local currencies, materials platforms like Materiom[47], 3D printing, maker and hacker labs and community kitchens. So much has been accelerated as a consequence of the

digital revolution. Some writers are publishing on the rise of the 'real sharing economy': 'Shareable Cities'[48] and 'How Non-Profits Will rule the World'. In living system terms, this is about the emancipation of the essential and productive 'periphery'. It is the *most of the apple tree* illustrated (figure 17).

Open digital networks are a natural hosting infrastructure for commons. They provide accessible, low-cost spaces for people to devise their own forms of governance, rules, social practices and cultural expression. That's why the Internet has spawned so many robust, productive information commons: free and open source software; Wikipedia and countless wikis; more than 10,000 open access scholarly journals; the open educational resources (OER) movement; the open data movement with sites for collaborative art and culture; Fab Labs that blend global design with local production; and much else. In an age of capital-driven network platforms such as Facebook, Google and Uber, however, digital commons must take affirmative steps to protect the wealth they generate.

Economies of scope (rather than scale) are "efficiencies formed by variety, not volume". They very often suit the devolved and distributed world not least because digital has made production and exchange more efficient for local producers and those with limited amounts of capital. The creation of multiple products/services and the multiple cash flows that result can lift overall income despite the smaller scale. Here it is not the large volume and large scale that matters but the effective local market, so that waste or by-product from a variety of sources can be sold into the immediate economy to become food for the system - on and on again using low transaction, limited investment and minimal energy costs. Gunter Pauli has contrasted very succinctly and carefully the difference

Figure 17 (left opposite page):

The apple tree's trunk and branches are 'structure and flow' while the twigs, leaves, filial roots and tendrils are 'exchange' focussed. The latter are the interface and they are the basis for creating the nutrients the tree needs

Credit: Tawng

between the two approaches. For him *adding value* rather than focussing on lowering costs is fundamental. It's about adding value to what is available. He is ebullient:

> "The Double Digit Growth Model:
>
> 1. Respond to basic needs
>
> 2. With local products and services, and
>
> 3. Circulate the cash in the local economy" [49]

In truth, it's not either economies of scope or economies of scale. There need not be anything more than a creative tension between these different approaches to value creation. And just as the big firms need customers, the precariat needs tools and connectivity and access to the commons. Digital technologies are central to both these economies of scope and scale which by design and intention, and with time and many failures, can evolve to produce effectiveness. *Neither efficiency nor resilience on their own give a good result*, only the appropriate relationship between resilience and efficiency provides effectiveness. As in all systems built by iteration, by feedback, the algorithm, the rules of the relationships are the key, as over time they give the sorts of patterns we desire or, they can be adjusted to do so. Sally Goerner's efficiency and resilience graph is repeated on the opposite page.

The shape gives a first clue. The curve is weighted, the diagram is skewed towards the resilience side. The bias is towards the network rather than the hierarchy, and oddly enough these patterns around scale are remarkably consistent. From organisms to cities and corporations, writer and scientist Geoffrey West[50] has been impressed by the regularity in which these systems scale and how they mark a general characteristic of all such systems. So why not the economy? Or to flip it around, we have to see an economy this way too.

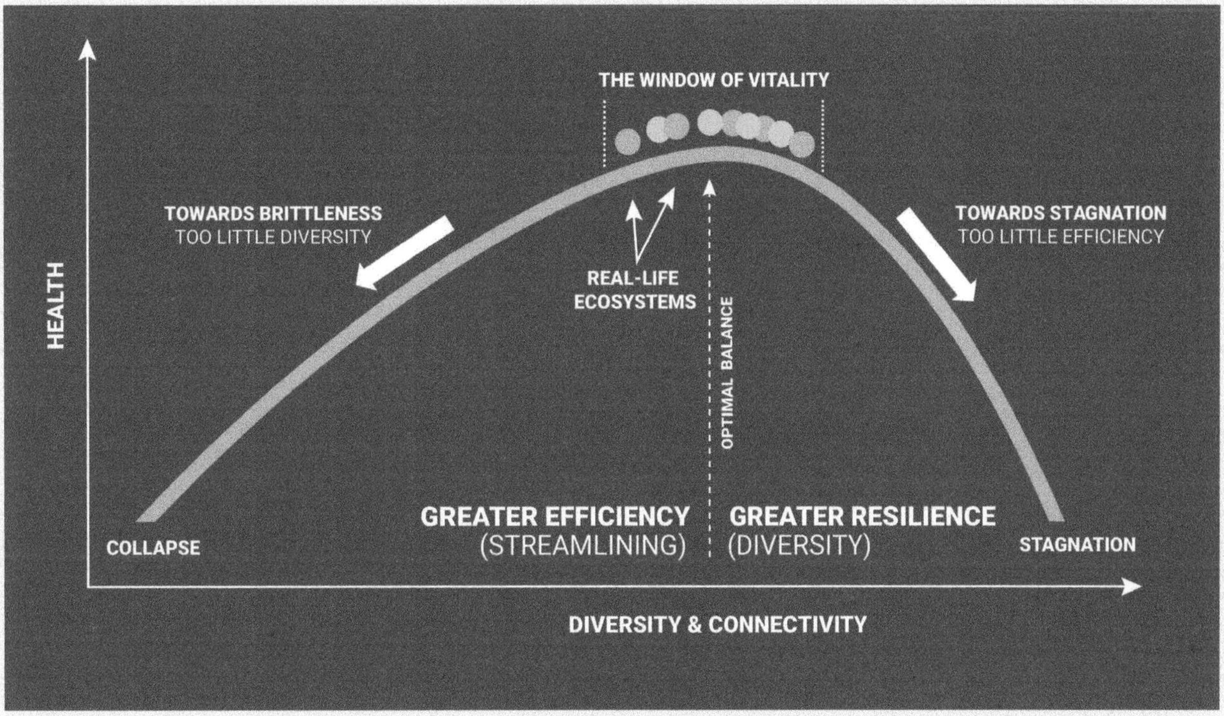
THE WINDOW OF VITALITY
TOWARDS BRITTLENESS
TOO LITTLE DIVERSITY
TOWARDS STAGNATION
TOO LITTLE EFFICIENCY
REAL-LIFE ECOSYSTEMS
OPTIMAL BALANCE
HEALTH
GREATER EFFICIENCY
(STREAMLINING)
GREATER RESILIENCE
(DIVERSITY)
COLLAPSE
STAGNATION
DIVERSITY & CONNECTIVITY

Figure 18: 'The Window of Vitality': why the health of a system needs a balance of efficiency and resilience

Adapted from: Sally Goerner, Bernard Lietaer and Bob Ulanowicz[9]

Illustration: Graham Pritchard

Adding value is about adding to resilience *through the development of many more nodes and connections* - it's about scaling out by propagation or replication (there are a lot of leaves on a tree). Adding value on the efficiency side is about *increasing throughput and efficiency scale* - here the price is a degree of rent seeking (there are not many large branches on a tree). If cities and corporations have similar scale relationships to a tree then perhaps this is more than a mere observation. It could be a clue to how to support the economy as a whole. Maybe the economy does not work optimally otherwise. What is less clear is the answer to this question about the economy: "whom do you serve?"

In the last episode of the imaginary we look at what is behind it all: we consider the conundrum of power, of control, in these different kinds of complex and dynamic economic systems.

6) Celebrate diversity and democracy in a transformative circular economy

We know that complex living systems are noisy, dynamic, diverse and indeterminate and throw up novelty. As a result, the system is creative and can evolve. Take a walk in any forest over the seasons and the years to sense this relationship. This is a big deal. Equally, living systems have a degree of stability – their many nodes and connections give a resilience that remains coherent over time (see the earlier discussion on panarchy and think here again of forests with their multitude of species connected together in food webs). How to achieve this stability and resilience in a diverse world of billions of decisions by billions of people and nearly as many communities is another wicked problem.

Democracy designed in the era of ballot boxes, mass production and consumption, limited literacy and national decision-making just looks as crude and lacking as does an economy designed as engineering pipework. In this introduction to the book's imaginary we have tried to show a renewed economy but it seems our ideas of democracy are as much in need of renewal[57]. Democracy has become so enfeebled with its once-in-a-while choices around parties and figureheads who often share the same economic understandings, the same theory and the same tired juxtapositioning of labour and capital. Instead, we need an 'active periphery' where more and more people participate in their own lives and communities, rather than as passive consumers dependent on work. Or as peasants or 'neoserfs' in the gig economy[46].

In a reinvigorated democracy people are consumers, producers, citizens and 'commoners', and increasingly urban and networked. Many are engaging in active citizenship through feedback-rich learning networks – so-called 'schools of democracy' in a phrase used by Michel Bauwens around the peer-to-peer

sharing economy. The commons is igniting grassroots development where residents regain power to make decisions, priorities and choices in a participatory manner. As Tommaso Fattori
suggests "it is this first person activity which changes citizens into
commoners".

Looking forward, we believe that, potentially, commoners could
have new freedoms and autonomy because of: the foundation of
an adequate basic dividend; access to historical and newly created
commons; the shift to renewables; business opportunities based
on turning waste into food; and access to money and credit provi-
sioning that suits them, secure in their right to do so.

Guy Standing[51] has made the case for celebrating and remind-
ing people of England's Charter of the Forest in 1217, 800 years ago.
Just as Magna Carta began the slow progress towards human
rights the equivalent document of the Charter of the Forests
reminds us about the commons – the forests in this case – as
sources of wealth and wellbeing to which we have rights of access.

This reminds us that freedom and autonomy are based on a
distributive-by-design expression. As Kate Raworth[52] says, this
economy will be "regenerative and distributive by design". It will
not be an economy that is a welfare handout – based on a reluc-
tant redistribution of income, or one that is orientated on the idea
that there are no commons to speak of.

A few concluding comments about the imaginary we've introduced in this chapter. The story of the new economy needs to
be based within: a 'systems' framework; the digital data and its
tools; the abundance and diversity of the earth's endowment; the
world's distributed renewable energy sources; the re-invention of
money; and an appreciation of and access to the historical and
ongoing commons. Then what we call civilisation can start to

Figure 19 (opposite): Forest as commons and a source of wealth and wellbeing

emerge in a new form. This transformative economy we imagine will be creative and more tolerant of others (tense anxious people do not make good neighbours!), while recognising that some tasks are better done at different scales – big ones, global ones too. After all, the economy is one process. As Eric Beinhocker says:

"....economics has painted itself as a detached amoral science, but humans are moral creatures. We must bring morality back into the centre of economics in order for people to relate to and trust it. All of the science shows that deeply ingrained, reciprocal moral behaviours are the glue that holds society together. Understanding the economy as not just an amoral machine that provides incentives and distributes resources, but rather as a human moral construct is essential, not just for creating a more just economy, but also for understanding how the economy actually creates prosperity"[53].

Economy = one dynamic process, two cycles, four principles of change for each.

A very brief set of system assumptions and how to approach resetting the rules:

0 The context is an earth symbolised by the circle, its living systems intertwined with the physical

1 The economy is regenerative and distributive by design, it's one iterative, complex adaptive and dynamic system which is symbolised by the Ouroborous – the snake-dragon eating its tail. It runs on renewables for the most part

2 **Cycles:** in the first cycle there is the materials stocks and flows wedded to knowledge/technology to create, then safely consume/use goods and services. In the second cycle there is the stocks and flows of money and the commons, some of it enclosed as real estate, land and other properties for which rent is due. Together these productive materials and money/asset cycles comprise the economy embedded in the environment and society

4 **principles for the productive materials cycle**: regenerate and restore capitals including natural and social capital; be biomimetic ('waste = food' and 'diversity=strength'); shift from selling goods to selling services or performance; optimise the whole system (be *effective* not just resource efficient)

4 **principles for the money/assets cycle:** create a basic dividend; implement a debt jubilee; build the commons and invest in productive infrastructure at all scales; shift taxes from renewables to non-renewables (shift taxes from people and on profits of production and sales to unearned income and mineral and fossil fuels)

0: 1 x 2 x 4/4

Does this fix everything? It's empowered by digital technologies and a revitalised democracy which is also part of the feedback cycle: effective productive systems at all scales are made possible and energised by collaboration and networks of socially productive people. Even so, these changes don't 'fix everything'. But they set the relationships around which iteration might progressively improve the chances of a thriving economy which is conducive to happiness, rather than an economy that degenerates capitals and democracy in a self-defeating slide into wealth extraction – while there is still time...

So here's a summary of a transformative circular economy based on earlier work[54] and some of the ideas that we've introduced in this imaginary:

*"Built increasingly on the endless flow of energy from the sun (**energy in surplus**) is an economy which transforms materials into useful goods and services endlessly (**'waste = food'**). This economy **builds capitals** and maintains them. Money is information which stimulates and coordinates the exchange of all things at all levels and so material is transformed (**money as credit rather than a medium of exchange**). To do this, **prices act as messages** and like the need for materials to flow cleanly, uncontaminated for them to become food for new cycles, prices **need to reflect the full costs** to do their job. Like all living systems, a circular economy is dynamic but adaptive and, if enduring, it will be **effective**, neither courting disaster by over-extending efficiency (**brittleness**) or too resistant to change (**stagnation**). It **celebrates diversity** – of scale, culture, place, connection and time – because a dynamic system is full of change, by definition, and thriving in such an environment requires diversity – a fount of **creative adaption**, a means of **resilience**, a source of redundancy or back-up. A circular economy is led by **citizens**, **business and enterprise of all kinds** within the 'rules of the game' decided by **an active citizenship in a flourishing democracy**."*

In the following chapters, food systems will be an important context for the illumination of this transformative circular economy. We'll argue that a universal basic dividend is a key to better, affordable food which optimises local systems: a basic dividend is effective rather than merely efficient. Effectiveness means looking at the whole system not just a part of it. To illuminate this, the apple has been chosen as an important focus in this book. It has been situated for centuries as one of the most adaptable of foods, grown in a multitude of settings with thousands of varieties, all sprung from human effort and ingenuity. Yet the apple is, in its industrial, efficient form so narrowly conceived that only around 10^{55} varieties dominate our shops and they are grown in limited and standardised ways to suit the mechanics of growing, picking and packing in the 21st century. Nowadays, the apple is an example of underused abundance, wasteful and narrowly conceived production and neglected by-products and additional cash flows – just because that's what producers are told the market demands. Set the enabling economic conditions right though and the specialist apple cultivar, or the large apple tree root stock is not just the latest food fad of the already well off, or an apple tree too big to manage – instead, these cultivars and rootstocks underpin exciting new economic possibilities of production, exchange and regeneration of natural capital (we'll look into '3-D apple orchards' later in the book).

This book is looking for clues to the next economic story and it weaves between the Apple as a symbol of our food and farming systems and perennial orchards, as well as a symbol of human knowledge, skills and insight. Through the challenge of making sure enabling conditions are right, it wraps around the basic dividend and the commons. All this is set within a transformative circular economy as an insight into circulating materials, an insight into changed metaphors, crucially, but also conceived as shifting to renewables and circulating spending power to the productive economy and to improving natural and social capital.

Chapter references and notes

1. Harari, Y. Sapiens. A brief history of humankind. Penguin/Vintage. (2011)

2. Werner, R. Shifting from central planning to a decentralised economy: do we need central banks? (2017)
https://professorwerner.org/shifting-from-central-planning-to-a-decentralised-economy-do-we-need-central-banks/

3. Hanauer, N., and Lui, E., Gardens of Democracy. Sasquatch Books. (2011)

4. Boulding, K.E. Ecodynamics: A New Theory of Societal Evolution. Sage. (1978)

5 Pettifor, A. Production of Money. Verso. (2017)

6. Lovins, H.,Wijkman, A., Fullerton, J. and Wallis, S. A Finer Future Creating an Economy in Service to Life. New Society Publishers. (2018)

7. Cabrera, D. and Cabrera, L. Systems Thinking Made Simple: New Hope for Solving Wicked Problems. Independently published (2016) http://crlab.us

8. Koestler, A. Janus: A summing up. Random House. (1978)

9. Goerner, S.J., Lietaer, B., and Ulanowicz, R.E. (2009). Quantifying economic sustainability: Implications for free-enterprise theory, policy and practice. Ecological Economics, 69, issue 1, pp.76-81
https://econpapers.repec.org/article/eeeecolec/v_3a69_3ay_3a2009_3ai_3ai_3ap_3a76-81.htm

10. Homer-Dixon, T. Complexity Science and Public Policy. (2010)
https://homerdixon.com/complexity-science-and-public-policy-speech/

11. Gunderson, L. and Holling, C. Panarchy. Understanding transformations in human and natural systems. Island Press. (2002)

12. Keen, S., Ayres, R. and Standing, R. (2019). A Note on the Role of Energy in Production. Ecological Economics, 157, pp. 40-46
https://www.sciencedirect.com/science/article/abs/pii/S0921800917311746

13. Boulding, K. E. Economics as a Science. McGraw Hill. (1970)

14. Hawkens, P. Ecology of Commerce. Harper Business. (2013)

15. Lyle, J. T. Regenerative Design for Sustainable development. John Wiley. (2008)

16. Pauli, G. Upsizing. Routledge. (1998)

17. Hawkens, P., Lovins A. and Hunter Lovins,L. Natural Capitalism. Earthscan. (1999) https://en.wikipedia.org/wiki/Natural_Capitalism

18. McDonough,W. and Braungart, M. Cradle to Cradle. Remaking the way we make things. North Point Press. (2002)

19 In the Cradle to Cradle 'defined use scenario', hazardous materials are defined as a function of toxicity and exposure. A chemical which is toxic for water-based organisms poses no hazard threat if it does not enter water systems. In reverse, it means that any substance which might end up in water systems has to be non-hazardous. The same principle would apply to soil-based systems - any substance which poses a hazard to soil-based organisms or bioaccumulates should not be brought out on soils. For example, many insecticides and herbicides are hazardous to soil-based organisms and mineral fertilizer-derived uranium is known to accumulate in the soil, but might also leach into ground and surface waters. Source: Mulhall, D., Braungart, M. and Hansen, K. (2013). Life cycle analyses. In: Achieving sustainability: Visions, principles, and practices. Rowe, D. (Ed.), 1, pp. 499-504. Macmillan.

20 See Ellen MacArthur Foundation website https://www.ellenmacar-thurfoundation.org/

21 For example, see the excellent six minute video by Dawn Danby on whole system design. Autodesk. https://ccjrnl.wordpress.com/2010/12/03/whole-systems-design/

22. https://en.wikipedia.org/wiki/Say%27s_law and also https://econpapers.repec.org/bookchap/elgeechap/13837_5f4.htm

23. Bezemer, D. and Hudson, M. (2016). Finance is not the Economy. Reviving the conceptual distinction. Journal of Economic Issues, 50
https://www.boeckler.de/pdf/v_2016_10_21_hudson.pdf

24. Kelton, S. The Deficit Myth: Modern Monetary Theory and the Birth of the People's Economy. Hachette UK. (2020)

25. The work of Elinor Ostrom https://blogs. lse.ac.uk/lsereviewofbooks/2012/06/17/ elinor-ostroms-work-on-governing-the-commons-an-appreciation/

26. Clark, J. B. The Philosophy of Wealth: Economic Principles Newly Formulated. Cornell. (1886)

27. George, H. Progress and Poverty. Sterling. (1879)

28. Gaffney, M. and Harrison, F. The Corruption of Economics. Shepheard-Walwyn. (2007)

29. Ryan-Collins, J., Lloyd, T. and Macfarlane, L. Rethinking the Economics of Land and Housing. Zed Books. (2017). Also Guy Standing's very good book Plunder of the commons. A manifesto for sharing public wealth. Pelican. (2019)

30. Foroohar, R. Makers and Takers: The Rise of Finance and the Fall of American Business. Crown. (2016)

31. Mazzucato, M. The Entrepreneurial State: Debunking Public vs. Private Sector Myths. Penguin. (2018). Also see https://time.com/4089171/ mariana-mazzucato/

32. Standing, G. How a basic income can battle the 8 giants of a faltering economy. (2019) https://www.weforum.org/agenda/2019/01/ battling-eight-giants-with-basic-income/

33. See for example The march of the zombies. (2016) https://www.econo-mist.com/business/2016/02/27/the-march-of-the-zombies

34. Video interview with Guy Standing, November 2017. https:// www.telekom.com/en/company/digital-responsibility/work/work/ video-interview-with-guy-standing-506526

35. Pettifor, A. The Case for a Green New Deal and How to Pay for it. Verso. (2019) https://www.versobooks.com/ books/3102-the-case-for-the-green-new-deal

36. Graeber, D. Debt the First 5000 Years. Melville House Publishing. (2014)

37. Turner, A. Between Debt and the Devil: Money, Credit, and Fixing Global Finance. Princeton University Press. (2015)

38. Steve Keen on a modern debt jubilee https://www.youtube.com/watch?v=ocQWs8Eteql

39. Kay, J. The Rationale of the Market Economy: a European Perspective. (2009) https://www.johnkay.com/2009/06/02/the-rationale-of-the-market-economy-a-european-perspective/

40. The Commons Transition Primer. P2P Foundation https://primer.commonstransition.org/

and http://wiki.commonstransition.org/wiki/Main_Page

Michel Bauwens argues that trans-national commons are especially needed to help align governance with ecological realities and serve as a force for reconciliation across political boundaries. Thus to realise the commons and deter market and state enclosures, we need innovations in law, public policy, commons-based governance, social practice and culture. All of these will manifest a very different worldview than now prevails in established governance systems, particularly those of the State and Market – we need new kinds of enabler governance (what Bauwens calls the 'Partner State').

For an introduction to the history of the commons also see the interesting Michel Bauwens podcast discussion with Gregory Landua of Planetary Regeneration podcast (from 7.10 to 14.23).

https://soundcloud.com/planetaryregeneration/planetary-regeneration-podcast-episode-20-michel-bauwens

41. https://www.newstatesman.com/politics/economy/2017/10/how-world-s-greatest-financial-experiment-enriched-rich

42. Video of Jeremy Rifkin on the Third Industrial Revolution https://medium.com/wedonthavetime/make-way-for-the-third-industrial-revolution-d95137293be9

43. https://www.mckinsey.com/business-functions/mckinsey-analytics/our-insights/where-is-technology-taking-the-economy

44. A two-part documentary detailing a two-week stay in Mumbai's Dharavi slum. https://www.telegraph.co.uk/culture/tvandradio/6990314/Kevin-McCloud-Slumming-It-Channel-4-review.html

45. Turner, J.F.C. Housing by people: towards autonomy in building environments. Marion Boyars. (1976)

46. Mason, P. Post Capitalism. Allen Lane. (2015) http://www.leftcom.org/en/articles/2016-02-21/post-capitalism-via-the-internet-according-to-paul-mason-%E2%80%93-dream-or-reality

47. Materiom provides open data on how to make materials that nourish local economies and ecologies. The platform supports companies, cities, and communities in creating and selecting materials sourced from locally abundant biomass that are part of a regenerative circular economy. https://materiom.org/

48. https://www.shareable.net/sharing-cities/

49. Pauli, G. and Kamp, J. Plan A. The transformation of Argentina's economy. JJK Books. (2017).

50. West, G. Scale: The Universal Laws of Life and Death in Organisms, Cities and Companies. Weidenfeld & Nicolson. (2017)

51. Standing, G. https://www.opendemocracy.net/en/opendemocracyuk/why-youve-never-heard-of-charter-thats-as-important-as-magna-carta/

52. Raworth, K. Doughnut Economics. Seven ways to think like a 21st century Economist. RH Business Books. (2017)

53. Beinhocker, E. The Origin of Wealth. Harvard Business School Press. (2006)

54. Webster, K. The Circular Economy. A Wealth of Flows. Ellen Macarthur Foundation. (2015)

Webster, K. and Johnson, C. Sense and Sustainability: educating for a circular economy. Ellen MacArthur Foundation/Terra Preta. (2010) http://www.c2c-centre.com/library-item/sense-and-sustainability

55. Apple varieties

https://www.worldatlas.com/articles/the-world-s-most-common-types-of-apples.html

56. Samuelson, P. Economics. McGraw-Hill. (1948)

57. For discussion on 'participatory and deliberative democracy' see the authoritative OECD publication: Innovative citizen participation and new democratic institutions: catching the deliberative way. OECD Publishing. (2020)

https://read.oecd-ilibrary.org/governance/innovative-citizen-participa-tion-and-new-democratic-institutions_339306da-en#page1

CHAPTER 2
THE FOOD SYSTEM OF OUR
FUTURE | THE ENABLING CONDITIONS

"There's a staggering gap between rich and poor in terms of wealth and income and therefore access to food".

Tim Lang[12]

The fundamental mistakes we make about food production and a 'regenerative' agriculture are perhaps not found so much in the activities of the producers themselves, or in the whimsy or concerns of consumers, as in the enabling conditions, or lack of them, that ramify across the economy at home and abroad.

This sense that the rules of the economic game are fixed, almost a law of Nature, makes them sound inapproachable, but they are not. A new food economy can be built underneath and around the existing system by resetting some basic rules, all of them unremarkable in their own way. Not attending to these basic relationships is to follow the false lights of the wreckers onto the rocks of the existing narrative by stressing 'product innovation', 'individual responsibility', 'values' and 'healthy choices' – rather than the systems narrative. It sounds very dramatic. Put another way: we know that complex systems are built through the 'iteration' of simple rules – we have seen this, for example in the murmuration of starlings - and realise that you only need to know the rules birds follow in relation to their nearest companions to reveal the secrets of this wheeling, beautiful almost magical flocking[1]. Compare that to actually seeing the entire flock and thinking "wow, how do they do that, it's impossible – who's in charge here?"

In the imaginary at the start of this book, we describe the current economy and its recent history as one of building up and then having reality undermine, a series of narratives – these narratives are the shared understanding of the basic rules of the game.

The emerging economy, however, will probably take many of its insights from how living systems work, how an organism works, and how the organism fits its ecosystem. It's that story of the woods and the trees again. This new economy is rooted in complexity science and its emphasis is on dynamic systems, which are able to evolve to be effective at all levels. It's about circularity, feedback and development based on improving the stocks of natural and social capital and increasing exchange. Author Richard Denniss notes "it's the shape of the economy not its size" which matters[11].

The new economy's shape in regenerative agriculture is familiar (chapter 3). Describing it as a shape doesn't sound like a solution.

Figure 20: Starling murmuration

Photo credit: Tony Armstrong-Sly

True. But it's risky to talk about solutions anyway, since 'solutions' sounds like an end point, a fix for the machine perhaps. On the other hand, to seek the fallout from a shifted mindset is like trying to discern useful patterns, a kind of something which is positive all round, a 'something' which arises from the interactions in the system. Christopher Alexander, the author of *A Pattern Language*[10], called it a "quality without a name." He claimed it was something that was recognised deep down as a quality almost like 'beauty' or 'wholeness' or 'truth'. Modernism and even the post-modern distrusts all of this so the idea of a search for the changing state of the whole is often dismissed. In practical terms, it's easier to find a single tool and use it with determination. But the early proponents of a circular economy for transition resisted this probably because they were often designers, architects or biologists who saw that the desired shape or form was down to a small number of important principles working to reinforce each other at the same time so as to give a positive direction which was durable[2,3]. In chapter 1 we identified four key principles for the productive materials cycle:

1. Regenerate and restore capitals including natural and social capital
2. Be biomimetic ('waste = food' and 'diversity=strength')
3. Shift from selling goods to selling services or performance
4. Optimise the whole system (be effective not just resource efficient)

It's possible to start anywhere with these principles – say resource efficiency – but if the positive cycle and coherence is the aim (that 'flock' sensibility...thinking back to the starlings[1]) it has to have an understandable wholeness. Then all four principles being in play seems to be something of a minimum. In our search for the desired shape of a regenerative, circular economy we might need more than these four principles. For example, in the context of the biological materials cycle, we also highlight some of the characteristics of complex adaptive systems: energy is key and it's usually derived from the flow of sunlight and the fluctuating stocks of carbon in soils, plants and animals, not the fossil fuel stocks. In chapter 1 we've also indicated how, as a system, 'diversity is strength', that the purpose of the system orientates around 'effectiveness' and that this incorporates both efficiency and resilience. So the structure of systems seems to matter and there are different emphases as a consequence at different scales (it's about 'exchange/resilience' as well as 'structure/flow' functions). In short, the dominant flows are energetic and the temporary negentropic structures of living things have recognisable broadly similar patterns or structures – energy flow networks, to paraphrase Sally Goerner[9]. These make for the the systems 101 which allows us to build on the basic insight or metaphor.

Boundaries are necessary for humans to comprehend anything and the problems in defining systems is in choosing a reasonable boundary - and it's very true here. So much discussion about materials – resources – seems to go on with only a nod to the other drivers of the economy: energy in surplus; money as credit; and the structure of systems. Indeed, as we have noted, the role of money rarely features outside business or project finance. Money is not in the dominant story about the economy. Then again, energy and system structures don't feature very much either! This exclusion of money as credit sounded strange and we saw that textbook economics insists that the banks' main role is in connecting savers and investors and acting as intermediaries, rather than banks, money and credit having a transformative, or active (endogenous) role in our economies. Such is the power of framing. Even governments in the post-1980s scenario have a limited and shrinking responsibility because the dominant narrative sees them as a source of interference when they move outside their accepted role of protecting the populace and enabling business.

So here's our take on how the four monetary principles (introduced in chapter 1) could interrelate to create the foundations for an effective local and regional, even national food economy. The role of the government and of money creation is prominent but within a setting where it has more of an enabling function for enterprise rather than a welfare net and as an enabler for public protection, rather than regulation. This general approach is to prejudice in favour of productive economy rather than a financial or an existing assets-based economy and to do two things: reduce the attractiveness of unproductive or 'rent seeking' activities; and to increase the potential activity in the productive economy, not least by reducing costs and/or increasing income there. The four principles we illustrate are all part of this attempt to re-orientate financial flows so as to increase the economic security and freedom of individuals through circulating income at the appropriate scale, rather than extracting it.

A *universal basic dividend* is important and needs to be built up over time, from a variety of sources as a share of the benefits of enclosing the commons as well as appropriate quantitative easing. This foundational income, leads to opportunities for individuals and families to get involved in local and social food production of all kinds. Sometimes described as 'venture capital for the citizen', the basic dividend can complement the *shift from taxes on labour and profit* on productive enterprise, to taxes on non-renewable resources, including land value, intellectual property and financial transactions. Yet the basic dividend is not dependent on the tax shift, it's a *dividend*, a share in the return on assets. Or, at the very least, as Guy Standing suggests, one could remove the unnecessary tax breaks enjoyed around assets at present[4].

This has the effect of lifting the employability of people, creating the time and opportunity for the establishment of productive enterprise while the tax shift discourages waste and the costly extraction of virgin raw materials. Many of these new enterprises will be not-for-profit or cooperative and the food economy can be an obvious prime beneficiary of both basic dividend and this tax shift because food production and, to some extent, food processing, is local, uses a lot of labour and demands place-specific knowledge and networks.

The debt jubilee is a contributor to personal security and the re-set of the system. Money no longer spent on debt service can be allocated elsewhere and those with no debts can then contribute additional expenditure into the economy. There is nothing specific here for food production – except that food is a necessity of life and with a debt jubilee expenditure on it is likely to increase. It is well understood that the ability to think more broadly and evaluate choice decreases with increase in economic insecurity so with debt jubilee a burden is lifted and enterprise potential encouraged. Call it the psychological angle.

There is also a need to *build new infrastructure, tools and the commons* for a devolving food economy. The digital and other tools that enable renewable energy, widespread information and knowledge, education and even kinds of manufacturing/remanufacturing/repair are ever more available and cheap. But the creation or facilitation of infrastructure for a devolved economy is often slow to catch up. A patchwork exists in some places but it's rarer for local or regional government to make this infrastructure a priority, yet. The kind of thing we have in mind here includes temporary food stores (*not* food banks) where surplus produce can be utilised or directly processed as a basis for developing skills and enterprise alongside, say, community kitchens, and a revival of the commons and community land (e.g. 'allotments +' see chapter 6).

Maker and software labs and local currency are all needed as compliments to this new infrastructure for the food economy. Adding value here, locally/regionally, where the loops of food consumption and production can most elegantly intersect seems obvious. The reason that this new infrastructure has to be created by an enabling or partner state is that most of these firms, enterprises and potential sole traders have no surplus capital nor are they likely to 'go to scale.' In short, they are a permanent pool of marginal businesses, and the capital for infrastructure is a sound investment, especially in an era in which borrowing costs for government are zero or negative.

Figure 21: Community kitchen

Photo credit: Adobe Stock Images

Here's another important principle for creating foundations for an effective local, regional and national food economy: *enable effective information exchange and learning*. This ensures people know about and can act on what is available locally through suitable non-profit or platform cooperatives around, for example, food assemblies or agricultural tool libraries. Perhaps even add a layer to the basic dividend in the form of community currencies which can only be spent and exchanged within the area, whether this is a city or some other agreed boundary[5].

The potential of these enabling system conditions, working together, is fairly easy to discern though imprecise: local and regional food production, processing, preparation and consumption would increase because a) costs have fallen compared to globalised food production – which, in future, bears the fuller environmental cost of production and transport and b) incomes at the base have risen, especially if taxes are taken off labour and productive profit and c) access to land and many more community workshops/kitchens and local markets have become available in the infrastructure. Then, not only do people have the freedom to spend more time on food, including production, preparing, sharing, selling and consumption, they can do it from the basis of a passion or as a contribution to skills development or from a reaction to relatively expensive internationally traded goods. It doesn't matter. The choice, the blessed choice, to say no to unhealthy, over-processed convenience food is no longer seen as an act of heroism in the face of a crowded day when the local food alternative is expensive, complicated and often time consuming. Having a local currency, provided as part of a citizens' dividend, also circulates new spending close to the community, and digital, of course, makes it seamless – perhaps local authorities can accept same for payment of local taxes? It's nicely circular of course. Food and farming enterprises, across the scale of micro and meso and perhaps macro levels will respond to opportunities when access to resources, including land of course, is easier; when production and selling is less onerous. As an example...

Working a day or less a week on a market garden might be fine whereas a full time work commitment to growing fruit and vegetables might not. And in the ideal situation, the overhead, the middleman is not there. He's designed out, he's dissolved by digital so that producer and consumer are connected directly again so as to improve margins to the former and slash the costs to the latter. This *disintermediation* is one key for success – declaring the middleman unnecessary – rather than just swapping, say, the conventional supermarket for a large online retailer.

This is to move from a dependency culture to an independency culture. Autonomy is the right word. Not separate but able to act more broadly, with more agency. Sure, the big food supermarket will still exist but, like Amazon, it's more likely to be based in the Cloud delivering everything else, and some more. But why should that matter, except to the purists? This is not, here at least, primarily a moral question, it's a practical one: how to create effective economic flows which invite people to join in rather than make the existing treadmill and compensatory consumption model ever more entrenched, whilst the loss of the local food web goes on apace. It might be said that a merely *efficient* system then becomes a more *effective* food system by operating now at all scales, rather than the local surviving alongside the large scale as a niche choice of the higher income groups.

This 'effectiveness' argument is the space for democracy of course. What we joyfully do for ourselves and for our own shared or collective arrangements is much more in the spirit of an inclusive democratic society than the better off inhabiting their glorious villages beyond the suburbs or in the urban hot spots – with their artisan bread shops, superb restaurants and organic growers. That's whilst the rest of society has to make do with various gradations of processed industrial food because it is at least cheap, in money terms, and because so many peoples' lives are fragmented and insecure but dependent, every part of it, on scrabbling for income in a market where they feel that they are either contract serfs or tremulous welfare recipients. All this even applies to the remnants of a declining middle class, who used to have good jobs once upon a time. Is it any wonder, in addition, that so many food producers who cleave to a regenerative and smaller scale farming approach, out of necessity or by values, usually live marginally. It's tough and has been so for decades.

It is true enough, surely, that the system conditions shape the outcome. The paradox of food, diet and health is that without access to tools, resources, infrastructure and effective income and currency (including credit) it is hard to see how food futures can improve for the majority of people. Unless, of course, economic growth picks up after the COVID-19 pandemic but without breaking fragile environmental limits, *and* if this growth brings with it an expanding rather than declining middle class, who will buy the better stuff and improve their life expectancy (and create all of those other positive spin offs). The prospects for this seem vanishingly low a decade and more beyond the 2008 financial crash, where for most, real incomes languish where they have been for decades.

The paradox of the times is that we have a cornucopia of food production systems, foodstuffs and food knowledge as well as a huge cross-cultural set of influences to draw upon. We have people who would like to participate. Yet many would often rather watch TV chefs and celebrities make food than get very much involved themselves. It is as if the world is so exhausting that we are satisfied, or just comforted with this (and so much more!) happening vicariously through the media. Arguably, this distance is a mark of a dependency culture, and one which shares consequently only the illusion of democracy: the ability for people to comment through social media on what they dislike and regret; and to make consumer choices but with a curious sense of entitlement in their relationships. The on-demand service economy reinforces this idea that "we want it hot and we want it now" – we live, as Doug Rushkoff says, with *Present Shock*. Rushkoff, in the book of the same name[6], contrasts the expectations of Alvin Toffler in *Future Shock*[7] that we would be "disoriented by a future that was careering toward us", with the idea that "we no longer have a sense of a future, of goals, of direction at all. We have a completely new relationship to time; we live in an always-on 'now', where the priorities of this moment seem to be everything. Wall Street traders no longer invest in a future; they expect profits off their algorithmic trades themselves, in the ultra-fast moment. Voters want

Figure 22: The snake-dragon[8]

immediate results from their politicians, having lost all sense of the historic timescale on which government functions."

This idea of patiently creating, perhaps co-creating, a good food life through adjusting the enabling conditions, reflecting on what has been achieved and drawing in not just voters but citizens and politicians to make adjustments may seem abstract and futures-orientated. But, going forward, if real participation in the food system is orientated around those who have both success and time to spare, then every systemic change listed above contributes to expanding the numbers who can experience both that feeling of accomplishment and of having time to spare. It's not charity either. After all, the systemic changes discussed here only reflect a response to the broader shifts that are happening in society: in employment's decline and with it the income tax base; in the digital arena, surprising us with change almost month to month; in new social networks; and, to bottom it all, the very real concern that businesses need customers and so customers need an income.

For sure, the system shapes the outcome. And in the food system of the future, circularity will be part of the insight that "the snake-dragon shall endlessly eat its tail to stay alive".

In the next chapter we'll dig deeper into regenerative agriculture, 'waste=food' and the other principles of the materials economy to illustrate how they relate to food and farming systems. We'll try to picture the materials principles of the circular economy working at farm scale – what we call 'Dream Farm'. Later, we explore regenerative food enterprise networks – individual regenerative farm and food enterprises cannot succeed in isolation. Later in the book we move on to take a city focus. There we reveal a number of city food utopias and illustrate how the four materials principles could work alongside the four monetary principles to enable the evolution of urban and peri-urban food and farming systems – nested within the wider transformative circular economy.

Chapter references and notes

1. Watch this computer simulation of flocking and see what happens when rules are changed or left out. It falls apart eventually, or quickly coheres.

https://www.youtube.com/watch?v=QbUPfMXXQIYA

2. Hawkens, P., Lovins A. and Hunter Lovins, L. *Natural Capitalism. Creating the Next Industrial Revolution.* Earthscan. (1999)

3. McDonough,W. and Braungart, M. *Cradle to Cradle. Remaking the way we make things.* North Point Press. (2002)

4. Guy Standing on tax breaks. Two minute video. Renegade Inc. (2019)
https://www.youtube.com/watch?v=-tOJXKcGzBU

Also see Guy Standing on universal basic income - good four minute interview clip (2017) https://www.youtube.com/watch?v=EkHV6bkycXI

5. Leitaer, B. The Worgl experiment, Austria In: *Currency solutions for a wiser world* . (2010)

http://www.lietaer.com/2010/03/the-worgl-experiment/

6. Rushkoff, D. *Present Shock*: *When Everything Happens Now.* Penguin. (2013)

7. Toffler, A. *Future Shock.* Random House. (1970)

8. Snake-dragon illustration from a late medieval Byzantine Greek alchemical manuscript https://en.wikipedia.org/wiki/Ouroboros#/media/File:Serpiente_alquimica.jpg

9. Goerner, S.J., Lietaer, B., and Ulanowicz, R.E. (2009). Quantifying economic sustainability: Implications for free-enterprise theory, policy and practice. *Ecological Economics*, 69, issue 1, pp.76-81

10. Alexander, C., Ishikawa, S. and Silverstein, *M. A Pattern Language.* Oxford University Press. (1977)

11. Denniss, R. *Curing affluenza: how to buy less stuff and save the world.* Black Inc. (2017)

12. Lang, T. (2020). Diet, health, inequality: why Britain's food supply system doesn't work. Jay Rayner interview with Professor Tim Lang. The Guardian

https://www.theguardian.com/environment/2020/mar/22/tim-lang-interview-professor-of-food-policy-city-university-supply-chain-crisis

CHAPTER 3

REGENERATIVE FARMING | THE SEARCH FOR DREAM FARM NETWORK 1.0

"The nation that destroys its soil, destroys itself".
Franklin D Roosevelt

THE SOIL FOOD WEB

Our soil teems with a multitude of organisms which provide the necessary work for healthy plants to grow free from disease, pests and infertility. These interconnected interactions and feeding relationships (quite literally "who eats who") help determine the types of nutrients present in soil, its depth and pH, and even the types of plants which can grow.

Earlier we introduced the thought that a regenerative local and regional food economy will need to take its insights from how living systems work: how an organism works, and how the organism fits within its ecosystem. So we can start to say that this new food economy needs to be rooted in complexity science with an emphasis on dynamic systems which have to be effective at all levels. It's about circularity, feedback and development based on improving the stocks, flows and exchanges of biological nutrients. It's about building social capital as well as profitable enterprises (the financial capital). And, of course, for our food economy, soil is the critical natural capital in the system (figure 23).

To get a better idea of how this new food economy might work let's zoom in and have a more detailed look at the farm-level system at work within a transformative circular economy. Later we can move to a drone's eye view of the wider food system level – that should reveal the bigger picture, the infinitely complex connections and patterns of the broader food system and its associated enabling conditions.

So what's the essence of 'regenerative' farming? Certainly we're clear that the regenerative farm sits within the biological nutrient cycle of a circular economy. Mention regenerative agriculture, in fact mention 'regenerative' anything, and the living systems metaphors flood in. Here the idea is that control is impossible but wisdom is necessary. Regenerative farmers understand what makes a farm ecosystem productive and how to encourage the right conditions, so as to optimise the farm's potential to create multiple cash flows. That's achieved by designing and setting up ('stacking') a wide range of farm enterprises that can harvest ('feed' on) the wealth of biological nutrients flowing through the farm landscape. The overall costs of the farm operation are shared between a multitude of such revenue and benefits streams - these *economies of diversity* add resilience but demand a lot of knowledge and skills to make them successful. The orientation of the farm is natural and social capital protecting, regenerative at

Figure 23 (opposite page): Elaine Ingham and the soil food web[1].

Photo credit: Soil Food Web Inc

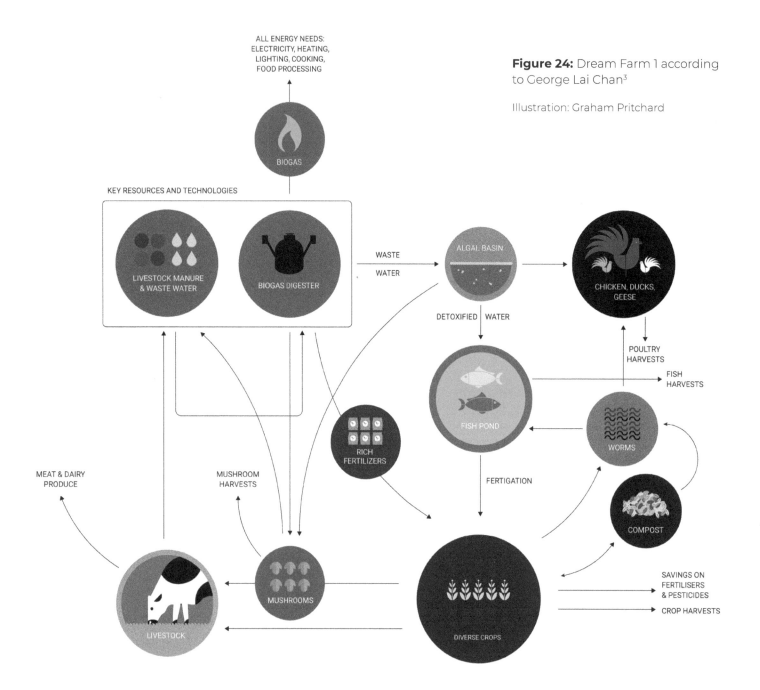

Figure 24: Dream Farm 1 according to George Lai Chan[3]

Illustration: Graham Pritchard

its best. Waste = food is a central principle at play on the farm so 'leaky' but nutritious loops are welcomed, they're not something to be avoided or designed out – everything is a resource for something else. The aim, consistently, is to design an effective farming system, not an efficient one, as we know that the whole is not only more than the sum of the parts – it's also necessary for the parts and the whole farm system to flourish long term: it's "feed the forest to feed the trees" again. The farm system works from top to bottom by evolving so that everything is food. It's built on soil bacteria and fungi in incalculable numbers, as well as on the oak tree and the owl. Healthy living soil is critical for success on this farm. Elaine Ingham, one of the leading soil ecologists in North America, puts the case that farm soils need to mimic the complex structure and diversity of soil found in natural forest and grassland ecosystems (figure 23, page 90).

Maybe we should try to visualise this regenerative farm with a story about 'Dream Farm' and the pioneering work of George Lai Chan and Mae Wan Ho – Dream Farm is an important early practical and theoretical regenerative farming model. Born in Mauritius in 1923, George Chan studied engineering at London University and spent much of his career in the South Pacific including the Northern Mariana Islands where he witnessed problems of poverty and sanitation on many of the small isolated islands. But it was over the period 1985-90, following his retirement, that he worked with small farmers living on the then agricultural Pearl River Delta in southern China. There he found the 500-year-old 'Dyke-Pond' region covering 80,000 hectares .Both the aquaculture in the deep fish ponds and agriculture on the elevated dykes surrounding the ponds were highly productive systems *without the need for external inputs* deriving from fossil fuels or artificial fertilisers. This is where, through careful observation, he developed his ideas around Dream Farm – or what he originally called the Integrated Farming and Waste Management System (IFWMS)[2]. Figure 24 shows how the integrated dyke-pond farm typically consists of crops, livestock and fishponds. But the nutrients from farm wastes often spill over (Bill McDonough's biological nutrient 'cascades') into supporting extra production of algae, chickens, earthworms, silkworms, mushrooms, and other valuable farm enterprises that bring additional income and benefits for the farmers and the local communities.

Chan confessed he learned just as much from these farmers on the Pearl River Delta as in his whole university career. He commented in his autobiographical notes: "we learned many lessons on how to do so much with so little, and why we should recycle all wastes and residues which were resources before... what an education it was!"[4]. What he learned was a nuanced system of farming and living that inspired him and many others, including Gunter Pauli, the influential founder and director of the Zero Emissions Research Initiative (ZERI).

Chan left China in 1990, and continued to work with Pauli and others in ZERI through consultancy services. This work took him to nearly 80 countries and territories, and contributed to evolving IFWMS into a compelling alternative to conventional industrial farming. In 2005 George Chan was in correspondence with Mae Wan Ho based at the Open University in the UK. They went on to work closely together to conceptualise the enhanced 'Dream Farm 2' model[5]. Developed as a theoretical model for use on both tropical and temperate farmlands Dream Farm 2 is a farm system par excellence designed around those important circular economy principles of "waste=food", "celebrate diversity" and "shift to renewables".

Because Dream Farm 1 and 2 are scalable and complex living systems, it's not essential to have all the farm enterprises operational at once. Evolved place-specific systems are key for success and these take time to develop. So it's possible to start with a very simple system consisting of biogas digester, livestock, crops and algae basins without fishponds, as that essentially does the water purification already. The algae grown in the farm's algae basins can be used to feed livestock, as an alternative to grain or soybeans used in the conventional industrial agricultural system. Later on, fishponds can be added and aquaculture and agroforestry enterprises can be 'stacked' on the pond dykes and surrounding farmland e.g. orchards and woodland. Additional income flows on the farm can come through poultry and mushrooms, as well as lots of fresh fruits and vegetables aimed at recovering indigenous biodiversity of both plants and animals. And conceptually at least, we have the gourmet restaurant on site to make good use of the fresh organic produce! Mae Wan Ho described the shift to renewables in this farm system:

"Dream Farm 2 consciously integrates food and energy production, emphasising consumption of both at the point of production...

solar power and wind turbines suitably scaled down can be installed, micro- hydroelectricity also in some locations. Combined heat and power generation is well developed. ...all this renewable energy harvesting would provide enough fuel for cars and farm machinery retrofitted to run on natural gas, as well as heat for the conservatory with more aquaculture and warm fishponds, where we can install water harvesting and water purification, again, based on well-tried technologies".

Fig 25: Oak woodland food web
Adapted from: Charles Krebs[6]

Illustration: Graham Pritchard

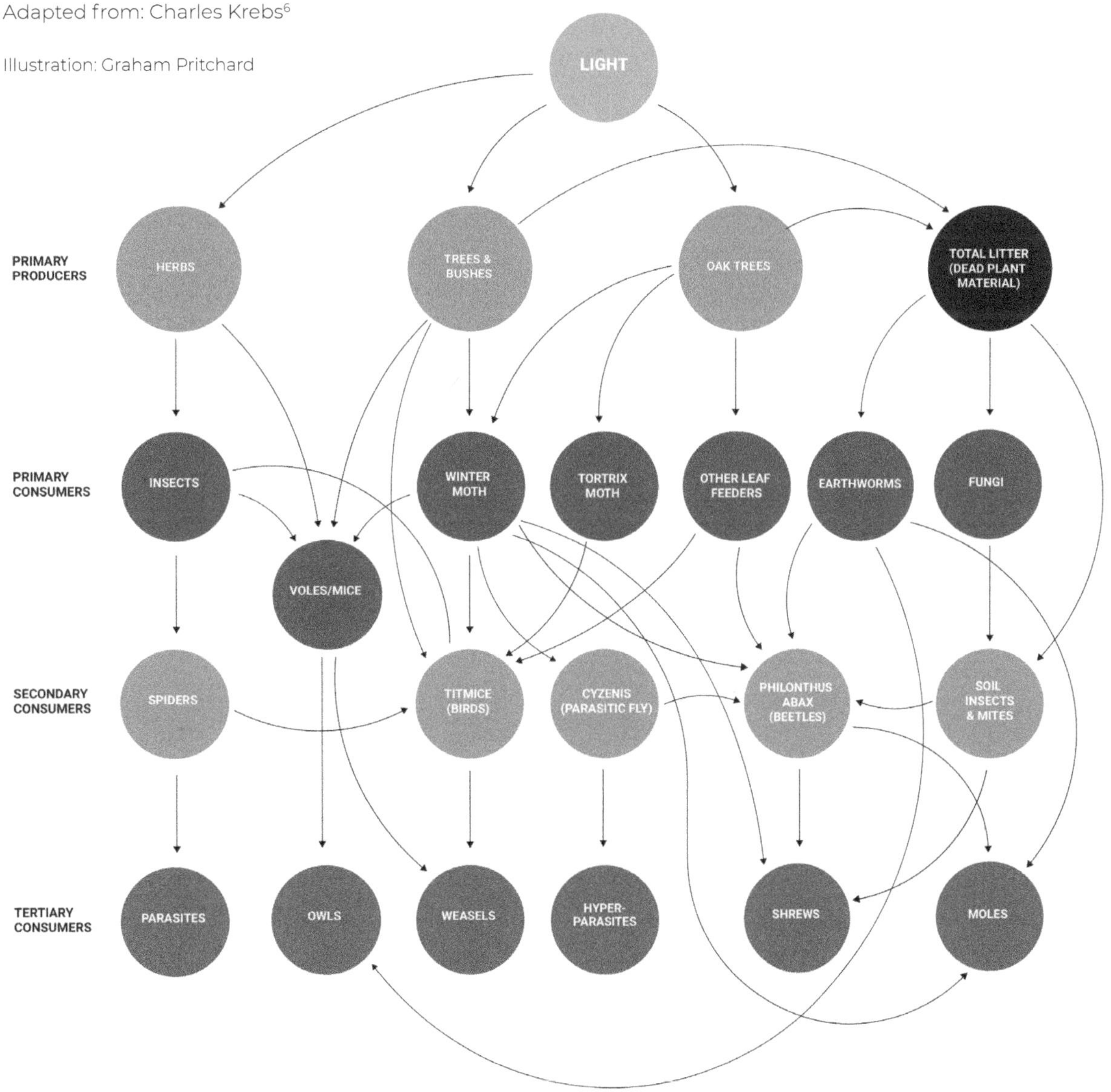

BOX 1
CRADLE TO CRADLE AND BIOLOGICAL NUTRIENT CASCADES

One of the first Cradle to Cradle projects was implemented in Brazil in the early 1990s. Drawing on insights from George Chan's Integrated Farming and Waste Management System (IFWMS) and other models, the goal was to cascade biological nutrients from communal toilet wastewater for agricultural production, while purifying the water for use in market gardening and farming. George Chan worked with Katja Hansen, Douglas Mulhall and the Hamburg Environmental Institute (HUI) in Brazil, Mauritius and China between 1992 and 1997. This included a 1 million Euro research project with HUI when the team designed and constructed three demonstration projects in Brazil and one at an experimental farm in Donguan, China. Extensive research showed how the biological nutrients could be used in a variety of products from biogas and compost for soil regeneration and improving growth of manioc (cassava), bananas and mushrooms, to feed for fish. These systems are now adapted for use across South America and the Caribbean.

Figure 26: 1930s Dustbowl, USA
Adapted from: Braungart, M., Hansen, K. and Mulhall, D. (1997)   Hamburger Umweltinstitut (2018) and Hansen, K. (2012)[19, 20, 21]

Photo credit: USDA

Notice that Dream Farm 1 and 2 is not a farm economy committed to economies of scale (it's no large-scale industrial monoculture). Its emphasis is on *economies of scope* – where a wealth of farm enterprises can generate diverse income streams from the flow of biological materials through the system. Dream Farm designs mimic structures and processes found in natural forests and freshwater wetland ecosystems – really the Dream Farm 1 illustration in figure 24 looks more like the species diversity and complex biological nutrient flows in a forest food web. In a complex natural ecosystem, like a forest, again the name of the game is economies of scope (figure 25).

Through their work, from the mid-1980s onwards, George Chan and Mae Wan Ho were early pioneers in the thinking about regenerative farming systems. Of course many other thought leaders and practitioners have influenced, or are currently influencing, the focus and development of regenerative agriculture. Some of those early pioneers in the 1930s rang an early alarm bell about the downside of industrial agriculture - the 'Dust Bowl' on the American prairies was caused by extensive soil erosion taking place across the vast farmland acreages in the USA. (figure 26)

The emergence of industrial agriculture took place on the American prairies from the 19th century onwards. It was the new railway transport system, from the 1850s, that enabled the westward expansion of wheat farms and cattle ranching across the prairies – the railways connected the vast grasslands with the growing cities and their markets on the East Coast[7]. Of course we know about the huge benefits achieved – large increases in wheat, beef and other farm crop yields. Yet the 1930s Dustbowl was an important prompt and wake-up call for the growth of the organic farming movement in North America and Western Europe[7]. Through the work of some of the early organic and permaculture farming pioneers and personalities – Eve Balfour, Henry Doubleday, Bill Mollison, Jerome Rodale and others – there was

BOX 2

SELECTED BOOKS FROM THOUGHT LEADERS AND PRACTITIONERS THAT HAVE INFLUENCED/ARE INFLUENCING THE DEVELOPMENT OF REGENERATIVE FARMING

Rudolf Steiner, *Agriculture: A Course of Eight Lectures.* (1924)

Rachel Carlson, *Silent Spring.* (1962) Houghton Mifflin

Eve Balfour, *The Living Soil.* (1943)

Bill Mollison, *Permaculture: A Designers' Manual* (1988) and *Introduction to Permaculture.* (1991) Tagari

David Holmgren, *Permaculture: Principles & Pathways Beyond Sustainability.* (2002) Holmgren Design Services

Allan Savory/Jody Butterfield, *Holistic Management: a new framework for decision-making.* (1999) Island Press

Joel Salatin, *You Can Farm: the entrepreneur's guide to start and succeed in a farmer's enterprise.* (1998) Chelsea Green

Elliot Coleman, The Winter Harvest Handbook: year round vegetable production *using deep organic techniques and un-heated greenhouses.* (2009) Chelsea Green

Martin Crawford, *Creating a Forest Garden: working with nature to grow edible crops.* (2010) Green Books

Nicolas Lampkin, *Organic Farming.* (1990) Farming Press Books

Christopher Alexander/Sara Ishikawa/Murray Silverstein, *A Pattern Language.* (1977) Oxford University Press

Richard Perkins, *Regenerative agriculture: a practical whole systems guide to making small farms work.* (2019) RP59'N

Joy Larkcom, *The Salad Garden and Oriental Vegetables: the complete guide for garden and kitchen.* (1991) Frances Lincoln

Vandana Shiva, *Monocultures of the Mind: biodiversity, biotechnology and agriculture* (1993) and *Stolen Harvest: the hijacking of the global food supply.* (2000) South End Press

Gunter Pauli, *The Blue Economy* (2010) Xlibris. and *The Third Dimension: 3D farming and 11 unstoppable trends.* (2017) JJK Books

Janine Benyus, *Biomimicry: innovation inspired by nature.* (1997) Harper Collins

a growing recognition of the critical importance of healthy soil for farming – that it was a complex and dynamic system teeming with life.....the thinking about the key principles underpinning regenerative farming was underway.

Box 2 gives just a taste of some of the researchers and farm practitioners now working in the field of regenerative agriculture and horticulture. Centres of excellence are emerging around the world. One of these is based at Coventry University UK where Michel Pimbert and his colleagues focus their research on the applicability of what they term 'agroecological farming' to small and medium scale farms in both tropical and temperate climates[8].

For Pimbert, 'agroecology' is based on the idea that farms should "mimic the structure and functioning of natural ecosystems." As he says:

"In ecosystems, there is no 'waste': biological nutrients are recycled indefinitely.... waste=food. Agroecology aims to close nutrient loops – returning all nutrients that come out of the soil, back to the soil....Agroecology also harnesses natural processes to control pests and build soil fertility. Agroecological practices include integrating trees with livestock and crops (agro-sylvo-pastoral farming), producing food from forests (agroforestry), growing several crops together in one plot (polyculture) and using locally adapted and genetically diverse crops and livestock."[8]

So Michel Pimbert takes us back again to some of those important principles for a circular materials economy discussed in chapter 1: be biomimetic so that waste = food; celebrate diversity; rebuild natural capital (such as soil). This should be unsurprising as they are core science not fashionable opinion.

That biomimetic design principle is key in agroecology and regenerative farming. Defining agroecology is important. A short definition? *Agroecology* is all about *agri*culture drawing inspiration from (mimicking) *ecology* and ecosystems. So, in a nutshell, agroecological farms are farms whose *agricultural* systems are designed and managed using insights about the structures and *ecological* processes that occur in natural ecosystems – such as grasslands or forests.

Michel Pimbert points out that small-scale farmers around the world implementing agroecology do so not only to produce healthy and nutritious food, regenerate soils, enhance biodiversity and adapt to climate disorder, but also to improve their income and working conditions by developing short food chains and local markets, thereby cutting out multiple middlemen. The agroecological model under development at Coventry University stresses the importance of local ecologies and economies being regenerated from below through an insistence on 'food sovereignty' (community control over the way food is produced, traded and consumed) and 'transformative' agroecology (as opposed to more watered down versions of agroecology, such as 'climate-smart', 'sustainable' or 'conservation' agriculture).

For us, Michel Pimbert's agroecological model and definition of agroecology currently provides the most detailed and appropriate definition of 'regenerative agriculture'. Bill McDonough and Michael Braungart in their book *Cradle to Cradle* advise that there are some things design innovators and business leaders can do to help steer the transition at every stage and improve the odds of success. One of their advices is "signal your intention". We like it that Pimbert clearly signals his intention. He commits to a new agricultural paradigm rather than to an incremental improvement of the old. With his agroecological model it's obvious that the intent is not to be slightly more efficient, to improve on the old model, but to fundamentally redesign the very framework of our agriculture and food systems. *Throughout this book we use the term 'regenerative agriculture' but we see it only as shorthand for Pimbert's elegant agroecological model with its focus on both the farm practice and food sovereignty dimensions.*

One of the clearest demands of the agroecology and food sovereignty movement is for citizens to exercise their fundamental human right to decide their own food and agricultural policies (the Nyéléni Declaration[9] for food sovereignty was made in 2007). Food sovereignty is indeed perhaps best understood as a process that seeks to expand the realm of democracy and freedom (social capital) by regenerating a diversity of locally autonomous food systems.[10]

Support for this kind of 'transformative agroecology' has come from an influential voice – José Graziano da Silva, former Director General of United Nations Food and Agriculture Organisation (FAO) who spoke at the 2nd International Symposium on Agroecology (April 2018):

"Today, the world still produces food mainly based on the principles of the Green Revolution. Most of this production is based on high-input and resource-intensive farming systems at a high cost for the environment. As a result, soil, forests, water, air quality and biodiversity continue to degrade. And this focus on increasing production at any cost has not been sufficient to eradicate hunger, despite the fact that nowadays we produce more than enough to feed everyone. In addition, we are seeing a global epidemic of obesity. This situation is unsustainable. We have reached an inflection point. We need to promote a transformative change in the way that we produce and consume food...Agroecology can offer several contributions to this process....agroecology transcends the farm, and provides many economic, social and environmental co-benefits. In fact, agroecology can improve the resilience of farmers, especially in developing countries where hunger is concentrated. It can contribute to boost local economy. It can safeguard natural resources and biodiversity, as well as promote adaptation to and mitigation of climate change...."[11]

It's clear that there is a wealth of regenerative farming and horticulture practitioners and researchers around the world putting this all into practice (box 2). Here are just a few of their top notes and advices for regenerative farm and market garden start-ups:

"Build income streams, stack your farm enterprises." The advice here is to draw down the multiple income streams from the crop harvests and added value enterprises, whilst at the same time regenerating farm soils. Richard Perkins and Yohanna Amselem run their small family farm, Ridgedale, up at 59' latitude in the north of Sweden. Up here it's cold and dark much of the year with

Figure 27: Ridgedale Farm, Sweden. Mobile chicken pens on pasture (foreground) follow sheep and cattle. Market garden with polytunnels and no-till raised beds.

Photo credit: Richard Perkins

a short growing season, yet this is one of Europe's most successful and well-respected regenerative agriculture businesses[12]. Many of the circular economy principles introduced in chapter 1 are at play here. Perkins' complex systems know-how shines through with his choices and phasing for farm enterprise stacking: market garden; pasture-fed chickens for eggs and meat; pasture-based sheep and cattle; on-farm meat curing; fruit and nut tree orchard; on-farm poultry processing facility; online and face-to-face courses for the next generation of entrepreneurial young farmers; and an online shop where tools and technologies used at Ridgedale can be purchased by market gardeners and farmers.

"Keep your farm livestock – cattle, sheep and chickens – on the move." Gabe and Paul Brown follow this advice on their 5,000 acre farm in North Dakota, USA[13]: "when the bison ruled the plains, they were followed by vast flocks of various birds, so we imitate this phenomenon on our own ranch. Our laying hens follow the cattle on pasture, free to roam while returning to the portable eggmobile to lay their eggs". For his cattle, Brown follows the 'holistic management' and 'holistic planned grazing' methodology developed by Allan Savory at the Savory Institute[14]. Holistic management seeks to regenerate farm grassland ecosystems by using farm livestock as a proxy and mimic for the wild herds of grazing ruminants that the prairies and savannas of the world co-evolved with and depend on. Due to the pressures of predation from leopard, wolf, lion and other carnivores, natural herds of herbivores such as wildebeests and bison form tightly packed groups that are continuously on the go, moving on and grazing the grassland in a pattern that is unlike conventional domestic livestock management. This natural herd action, moving in 'pulses' across the landscape, results in a trampling and nutrient enrichment process of the soil (from the herd urine and faeces). That's essential for healthy grass growth and soil regeneration with effective nutrient and water cycling/distribution across the grassland. It's the abundance, not the paucity, of these grass-eating animals that the world's natural grasslands (savannas, prairie) remain healthy. Thus, holistic management recognizes that fully functioning grassland ecosystems cannot be maintained without herds of grazing animals.

Figure 28: Cows queue to enter an open air dairy for milking Photo credit: Tom Foot/The Open Air Dairy

"Build diverse and resilient infrastructure and land partnership models." In regenerative farming systems this is an important way to get added value enterprises based around the farm's crop harvests. But here the advice is to start to move away from the capital-intensive permanent infrastructure. Think differently, and design in low-cost infrastructure. Tim May[15], one of the U.K.'s leading holistic management and grazing practitioners, is about to set up one of Europe's first mobile milking systems[16] to follow his cows around the fields, rather than bring them back to the farmyard to be milked (figure 28). This leaves cow manure and urine behind to fertilise the pastureland. In this next-generation organic dairy farm, 400 cows will be milked in the fields as the animals simultaneously graze and fertilise their herb-rich pastureland.

Tim May has also established what is known as a 'share farm' land partnership model[27] with a young first generation farmer. As the landowner, he gives access to the land and the young farmer supplies the labour and machinery, including the mobile milking parlour. Both parties share the cattle and the running costs and then share out income from milk sales according to how much money (or benefits in kind) each has put in.

Marcus Link[23] has observed how in the conventional thinking about economies of scale, it is generally assumed that bigger will also be better, and so an approach to agriculture has developed – favoured by subsidies and financial institutions – which pursues large size, large yield and high efficiency. Yet the regenerative agriculture pioneers like Tim May, Gabe Brown and Richard Perkins challenge this approach and instead realise the need to farm with nature, not against it – that way of thinking, says Marcus Link, has led them to "*the concept of pursuing profit per acre instead of yield of pounds per acre* – the key to increasing profit per acre is diversity, grounded in biodiversity leading to diversity of enterprises". Put another way, the context for their business model is regenerated soil with increased biodiversity and carbon storage. That soil is the bedrock, the natural capital, on which to build many nested enterprises that together seek to maximise profit per hectare. In 2018, Brown counted 17 enterprises on his farm and was looking forward to adding many more[25]. In 2019, Perkins documented 13 enterprises at Ridgedale Farm with impressive financial detail on their profitability[24].

So there's an important conclusion to draw from the work of leading regenerative farm practitioners such as those highlighted in box 2: we have good proof of concept for regenerative farming. These are the practitioners at micro and meso-scale who at the *farm-scale* level, know how to successfully implement regenerative technologies and systems and to use them to run enterprises – at profit[29]. However, regrettably, in regions such as Europe and North America, it seems there is still little evidence, on the ground, of small/medium-sized regenerative farms and market gardens scaling out at fast pace[26]. It seems that the enabling system conditions which create the 'ecology of businesses' are not yet in play. When we now have the knowledge, technologies and proof of concept for farm-scale regenerative agriculture, why hasn't it taken off? Why can't we scale it?

In developed countries it seems to be a case of isolated regenerative farms trying to survive in an ocean of monoculture industrial farming. In developing nations much denser networks of small scale regenerative farms so far still exist but likewise they struggle to thrive within the industrial agricultural landscapes that dominate the world's fertile farmlands... A morass of linear economy disabling conditions so often prevent the growth of regenerative agriculture. For example:

• Regenerative farming systems are complex dynamic systems so they are a challenge to manage (compared to industrial monocultures). It is a challenge to set up, learn about and develop experience with diverse regenerative agriculture enterprises. The regenerative farmer strategises and adapts rather than box ticking "this is what we do". She is self-critical, multidisciplinary and, most importantly, tolerant of complexity – she is someone who sees the universe as complicated maybe to the point of many fundamental problems being unsolvable or inherently unpredictable. But a big part of the problem is that currently our school systems just don't encourage such systems thinkers. So many of our schooling systems are setting quite another direction, entrained by the understanding that thinks, incorrectly, the world is a machine-like affair and knowledge means just specialism and more knowledge, ever more of it.

- The corporate capture of the regenerative farming/agroeco-logy idea has been identified as another important disabling factor preventing the scaling out of regenerative farms. Michel Pimbert is very aware of this: ".. as (agroecology) gains ground and attracts the interest of mainstream institutions, it is now being recast as one of many possible 'innovations', alongside high-tech solutions like gene-editing, automation and big data. This often serves to strip the politics of agroecology away, reducing agroecology to a technical practice rather than a radical process of social-political transformation."[8]

- Food from these regenerative agriculture and horticulture businesses tends to be more expensive than conventional food so it is hard to generate a demand and market for these food products and services. Why? The application of economies of scale with cheap mechanical and energy capital inputs against a simplified (monocultural) agricultural and horticultural system reduces costs – typically, the real costs of those capital inputs are not factored in (i.e. there's no 'true cost account-ing'[22]) Nor is there consideration of the depletion of the nat-ural capital which is the soil. Add in the consequences of too cheap capital inputs across the food processing chain and the result is what we know – 'cheap' industrial food. But let's not call it cheap? Add in the issue of rents: more productive land is likely to attract and be able to support larger rents anyway (that's a plus for the larger wealthy landowner rather than the small regenerative farmer who can't afford those rents). To overcome such disabling conditions, the focus for small scale regenerative farming needs to become the additional reve-nue the farm gets from multiple enterprises/cash flows. Then, provided value can be added near to the farm (if processing is a reasonable price on a small or medium scale) and the farm can get around the traditional mark-up that middlemen take, then a living becomes possible for the regenerative farmer. And in future, customers could be in a stronger position to afford to support regenerative enterprises – provided, as discussed in chapter 1, they are now better off through more income e.g. from the return of the benefits of enclosure as a basic dividend.

Left: a pig raised in an apple orchard

One thing is for sure. Going forward, we have to be clearer about the differences between 'scaling up' and 'scaling out' business organisations. For us, healthy growth is about the successful scaling out of regenerative agriculture and horticulture enterprises within distributed local and regional food networks. In future, we need to think network, not just farm. These food enterprises need to grow outwards like fungal networks in a forest soil, rather than scaling up, getting bigger in size, growing upwards. This is about the search for local food networks thriving as complex dynamic and living systems. For success at the local and regional scales, we need to be thinking about a complex mosaic of food producers (different sizes, different business types etc.), land (varying land usership/ownership models, the 'commons' etc.) and food consumers connected in distributed (rather than centralised) food networks/ecosystems. In our view, to successfully scale out, the stocks and flows of biological nutrients and energy sources need to be carefully designed into the wider system – beyond the farm scale. Of course, monetary value creation and distribution and social capital building also need to be factored in for these regenerative food enterprise ecosystems – it's about rethinking enterprise – recognising that business is full of diverse interests, not all of them selfish, not all of them financial. These of course are economies of scope, not economies of scale. Chris Perley[17] observes that "in systems theory, you never do one thing. And if you're not looking at what else you've done with any act – economically, socially and environmentally – then the analysis (well, synthesis) is incomplete. That is an understatement. To see potential *scope* requires a mind that sees (and imagines) curves not lines, tangents, patterns and connections – across and within social, biophysical and economic domains. It ought to be the part of any 'professional' to be able to imagine – to induce, not deduce – beyond the constraints of a mechanical mind."

The chapter's conclusions: we know that regenerative agriculture and horticulture tools, technologies and infrastructure work at farm-scale but so far there is little evidence of scaling out: to successfully develop and grow, small and medium-sized regenerative enterprises need to develop within a healthy distributed enterprise network. Note again the parallel here with the resilient, exchange-based features and processes of living organisms or ecosystems – in the blood system of mammals or birds for example – where exchange of nutrients and waste materials takes place at the minute blood capillary/cell level of the system (see figure 7). Similarly, this level of the system is where the bulk of the economic action should always reside – provided the idea of 'economy' can escape the notion of it being just a purely monetary phenomenon.

Finally, we should return again to the pioneering work of George Chan. At the end of his life in his birthplace, the island of Mauritius, George Chan confessed: "I have dedicated my life to helping the poor and neediest of this world to transform their waste into wealth... And here I am almost ninety years later, forgotten and left in an old people's home."

This is very sad. And if it says anything, it is that having the theory and the practice and the success of regenerative farms does not mean others are ready or even prepared to listen. Or, perhaps, that the system conditions, the macro economics, are not working in the same direction or, indeed, that the existing linear economy narrative has not failed sufficiently to lead active minds to consider these other fertile ideas.

Rather than the search for George Chan's and Mae Wan Ho's Dream Farm 3.0, perhaps it's more about a search for local and regional clusters of regenerative farms, market gardens and other food enterprises nested together within a 'Dream Farm Network

1.0'? And these networks are a particular kind of network. They includes farmers on their farms and market gardens linking together, sharing practice and problems, learning about regenerative technologies etc. But to quote George Monbiot, journalist and author of the influential book *Out of the Wreckage*[28], the priority now is not 'homogenous bonding networks' (it's not about one million plus followers bonding together on a celebrity Twitter feed) but what he calls 'bridging networks' – networks made up of very diverse kinds of organisations and people, bridging rather than bonding together... farmers bridging with other food enterprises, local enabling government and of course farmers bridging directly with food consumers. In the next chapter we need to dig a little deeper into food and farming bridging networks.

Chapter references and notes

1. Ingham, E., Moldenke, A. and Edwards, C. *Soil biology primer*. Ankeny, Iowa, Soil and Water Conservation Society, in cooperation with the USDA Natural Resources Conservation Service. (2000)

2. Chan, G. L. (1993). Aquaculture, Ecological Engineering: Lessons from China. *Ambio*, 22, No. 7, pp. 491-494

3. Mae, W. H. *How to beat climate change and post-fossil fuel economy* http://www.i-sis.org.uk/DFHTBCC.php

4. Garcia-Dory, F. *George Chan. Dream farms*. Introduction by Fernando Garcia-Dory. 100 notes-100 thoughts series, number 051. Hatje Cantz. (2011)

5. Mae, W. H. *Dream Farm 2 - story so far*

http://www.i-sis.org.uk/DreamFarm2.php

6. Krebs, C. *Ecology. The experimental analysis of distribution and abundance*. Harper International. (1978)

7. Steel, C. *Hungry City*. Vintage Books. (2013)

8. Pimbert, M. (2017). Agroecology as an Alternative Vision to Conventional Development and Climate Smart Agriculture. *Development*, 58, No. 2-3, pp. 286-298

https://dx.doi.org/10.1057/s41301-016-0013-5

Anderson, C., Bruil, J., Chappell, M., Kiss, C. and Pimbert, M. *Agroecology now! Transformations towards more just and sustainable food systems*. Palgrave Macmillan. (2021). https://www.palgrave.com/gp/book/9783030613143

Also see: Giles, J. *The fight to define regenerative agriculture* (2019). Considers corporate capture of regenerative agriculture - the potential role of certification systems to address this matter https://www.green-biz.com/article/fight-define-regenerative-agriculture

9. Nyéléni Declaration https://nyeleni.org/spip.php?article290

10. Pimbert, M. *Towards food sovereignty.* IIED
(2010)   Downloadable at https://www.iied.org/
towards-food-sovereignty-reclaiming-autonomous-food-systems

11. 2nd International Symposium on Agroecology: *Scaling up Agroecology
to achieve the SDGs.* Mr José Graziano da Silva, Director-General, Food
and Agriculture Organization (FAO) Opening Plenary April 3 2018.

12. Perkins, R. *Regenerative agriculture – a practical whole systems
guide to making small farms work.* RP59'N. (2019)

Also see: Richard Perkins You Tube channel: https://www.youtube.com/
user/mrintegralpermanence

13. Gabe and Paul Brown ranch, Dakota https://brownsranch.us/

Also see: short films on 'Soil carbon cowboys' https://carboncowboys.org/

14. *What is holistic planned grazing?* Savory Institute website (2017)
https://www.savory.global/wp-content/uploads/2017/02/about-holis-
tic-planned-grazing.pdf

Savory Insitute Resource Library at https://savory.global/
resource-library/?utm_source=ActiveCampaign&utm_medium=e-
mail&utm_content=%F0%9F%93%95Savory+s+new+Resource+Li-
brary+-+just+launched%21&utm_campaign=Resource+Library

15. Tim May profile https://www.agricology.co.uk/field/farmer-profiles/
tim-may

https://www.kingsclere-estates.co.uk/

Also see: Akehurst, N. (2021). Growing potential. *South East Farmer*
https://www.southeastfarmer.net/section/features/growing-potential?f-
bclid=IwAR3topDcl4urj8tALRfPstLdlLsxKF0ZuT7W2wIbWVA1Pdyrst-
V2pCpDPKA&s=03

16. The Open Air Dairy - Tom Foot and Neil Grigg _http://www.openair-
dairy.co.uk/about-us/

17. Perley, C. *From Land as Factory, to Land as System: Realising the Potential that the Factory Technician cannot.* (2019) https://chrisp-erleyblog.com/2019/06/07/from-land-as-factory-to-land-as-system-realising-the-potential-that-the-factory-technician-cannot-see/amp/?__twitter_impression=true

18. Monbiot, G. *The new political story that could change everything* TED Summit (2019). 'Bridging networks' at 13.00 in the video https://www.ted.com/talks/george_monbiot_the_new_political_story_that_could_change_everything?language=en

19. Braungart, M., Hansen, K. and Mulhall, D. (1997) Biomass Nutrient Recycling - An affordable closed-cycle process with added benefits. Article from *Water, Environment & Technology.* http://www.c2c-centre.com/sites/default/files/Biomass-Nutrient-Recycling-EPEA_0.pdf

20. Hamburger Umweltinstitut. (2018). *Guide to wastewater recycling in tropical and subtropical regions. How to plan, build and operate waste-water recycling facilities in warm climates.*

http://www.hamburger-umweltinst.org/en/content/biomass

21. Hansen, K. *The Cradle to Cradle concept in detail (with Brazil case study).* Film 20 minutes length. Ellen Macarthur Foundation/University of Bradford. (2012) https://www.youtube.com/watch?v=HM20zk8WvoM

22. For a helpful article on true cost accounting see: Holden, P. (2013). True cost accounting in food and farming. *The Ecologist* https://theecologist.org/2013/nov/29/true-cost-accounting-food-and-farming

23. Ken Webster and Marcus Link, pers. comm. Marcus Link is a Founding Partner of New Foundation Farms https://newfoundation.farm/#about

24. Ridgedale Farm, Sweden - financial overview of enterprises (annual). Source: *Regenerative agriculture: a practical whole systems guide to making small farms work.* Richard Perkins. RP59'N. (2019) *excludes fixed costs, buildings etc.

Enterprise	enterprise revenue	enterprise running cost	enterprise net (euros)
Silvopasture	73,340	9,910	65,430
Tree nursery	75,460	21,180	54,280
Oyster mushroom	55,070	10,707	44,363
Forest raised pork	68,000	18,131	49,869
Pastured broilers	73,697	20,743	52,954
Pastured turkey	79,431	26,406	53,025
Pastured layers (eggs)	108,423	51,605	56,818
Pastured micro dairy	76,786	27,242	49,525
Pasture-raised lamb	116,740	67,345	49,395
Pasture-raised beef	81,201	37,444	43,756
Pasture-raised veal	82,456	38,714	43,742
Market garden	53,779	7,640	46,482
Micro greens	62,.480	12,584	49,896

25. Interview with Gabe Brown about his book *Dirt to Soil: One Family's Journey Into Regenerative Agriculture.* Chelsea Green. (2018)

https://www.sustainabilitymatters.today/gabe-brown-transcript

26. Currently little evidence on the ground of regenerative farming scaling out at fast pace. However, there are very hopeful signs this is about to change in Europe - see European Union strategies and target for 25% organic/agroecological farmland by 2030 https://www.ifoam-eu.org/en/news/2020/05/20/press-release-ifoam-eu-welcomes-landmark-decision-put-organic-heart-future-european

But see this agroecological critique of the EU *Farm to Fork* strategy https://foodgovernance.com/2020/06/05/eu-farm-to-fork-strategy-collective-response-from-food-sovereignty-scholars/2/

27. For discussion on 'share farms' see *The Land Partnerships Handbook. Using land to unlock business innovation.* (2015) Fresh Start Land Enterprise Centre.

http://freshstartlandenterprise.org.uk/wp-content/uploads/2015/07/LP-Handbook-2nd-Edition-Final-Print-Web-Version.pdf

28. Monbiot, G. *Out of the wreckage: a new politics for an age of crisis.* Verso. (2017)

29. Ploeg, van der J.D. et al. (2019). The economic potential of agroecology: empirical evidence from Europe. *Journal of Rural Studies,* 71, pp.46-51

https://www.researchgate.net/publication/335996382_The_economic_potential_of_agroecology_Empirical_evidence_from_Europe

Jan Douwe van der Ploeg and colleagues have detailed how, in Europe, agroecological farming can generate farm incomes that exceed those from conventional and industrial farms. He notes the enormous potential to further strengthen the economies of agroecological farms through the construction of closely knit networks for local processing and marketing.

CHAPTER 4
REGENERATIVE FOOD ENTERPRISE NETWORKS
3-D APPLE ORCHARDS AND OCEAN FARMS

*"The next agricultural revolution is about growing affordable,
nutrient-dense food on regenerating soils at scale".*
Mark Drewell, New Foundation Farms[31]

Figure 29: 'Nested market' of food enterprises, Netherlands

Adapted from: Jan Douwe van der Ploeg[1]

Illustration: Graham Pritchard

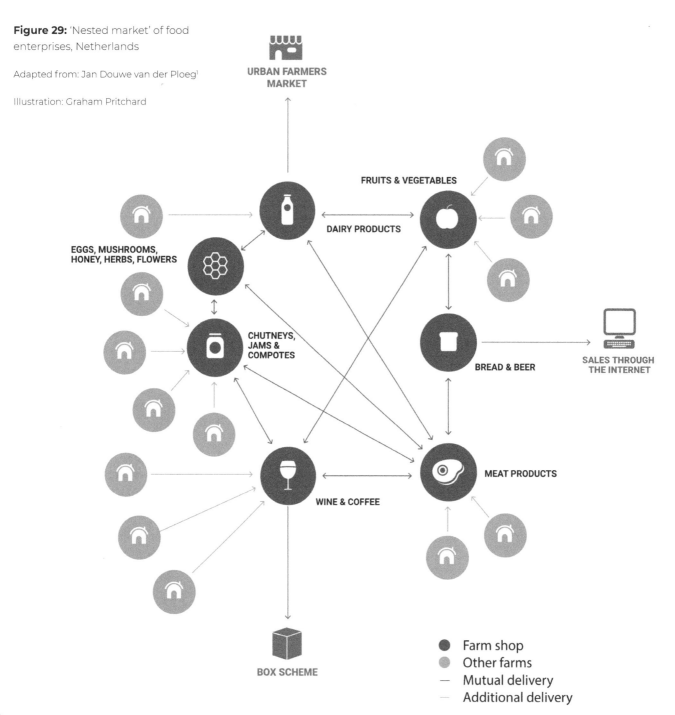

URBAN FARMERS
MARKET

FRUITS & VEGETABLES

DAIRY PRODUCTS

EGGS, MUSHROOMS,
HONEY, HERBS, FLOWERS

CHUTNEYS,
JAMS &
COMPOTES

BREAD & BEER

SALES THROUGH
THE INTERNET

MEAT PRODUCTS

WINE & COFFEE

BOX SCHEME

● Farm shop
● Other farms
— Mutual delivery
— Additional delivery

Earlier we suggested that regenerative food enterprises cannot succeed in isolation. To be successful, they need to be nested and scaled out within wider regenerative food enterprise networks.

This remark from a former US president seems to be doing the rounds of the systems thinkers. Dwight Eisenhower's advice? "If a problem cannot be solved, enlarge it." Expanding the boundaries of the problem uncovers new options, synergies and solutions – the question begging here is which boundary? Which of all these nested real world systems is the appropriate place to find new options and solutions?

We could perhaps make a start with this systems 'boundary expanding' by zooming out from the individual farm to an aerial view of nested food enterprises in a regional food system. Here's an illustration of a 'nested market' of food enterprises in the Netherlands, where like in many countries in Europe the direct selling of food (from producer to consumer) represents a major and quickly growing nested market. In Netherlands there are at least 2,300 farms participating in this direct selling that together achieve sales totaling at least €75 million. Within this network there is a subgroup of 85 certified farm shops (landwinkels). These are attractive shops constructed within the farm building and together they total sales of €16 million. During the last decade these farm shops have increasingly been interconnected in local networks (see figure 29) which allow a considerable enlarge-ment of the total range carried by each shop, thus making them more attractive to consumers whilst they also enlarge the sales per farm far beyond the limits of the locally available consumers. Jan Douwe van der Ploeg from the University of Wageningen has studied these nested markets and notes: "the building blocks are simple: local farm shops, small trucks with cooling facilities, inter-net, transparency and trust. Together, these ingredients construct a socio-material infrastructure that strongly supports the nested market in which these farm shops operate. It is infrastructure that functions as a *counter-structure* ...to the wider industrial food system".[1]

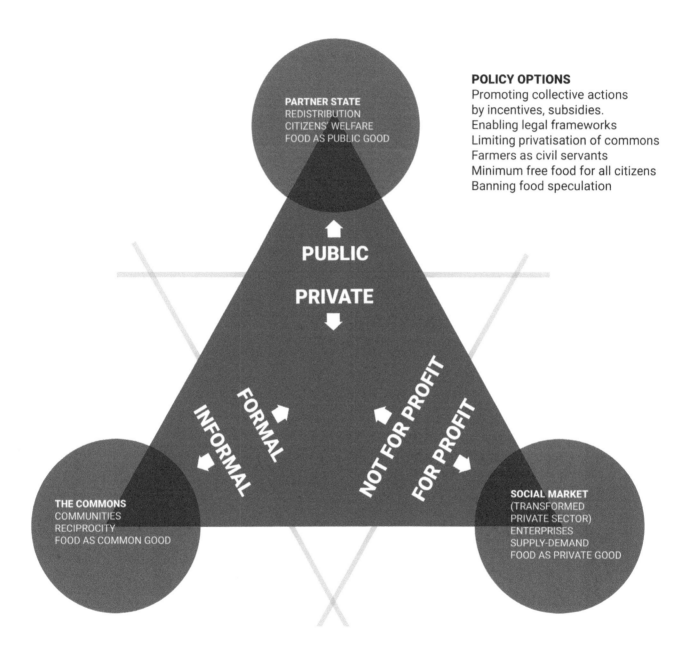

PARTNER STATE
REDISTRIBUTION
CITIZENS' WELFARE
FOOD AS PUBLIC GOOD

POLICY OPTIONS
Promoting collective actions
by incentives, subsidies.
Enabling legal frameworks
Limiting privatisation of commons
Farmers as civil servants
Minimum free food for all citizens
Banning food speculation

PUBLIC

PRIVATE

FORMAL

INFORMAL

NOT FOR PROFIT

FOR PROFIT

THE COMMONS
COMMUNITIES
RECIPROCITY
FOOD AS COMMON GOOD

SOCIAL MARKET
(TRANSFORMED
PRIVATE SECTOR)
ENTERPRISES
SUPPLY-DEMAND
FOOD AS PRIVATE GOOD

But let's expand those system boundaries again in this attempt to seek out new perspectives and solutions – think beyond just a network of nested food enterprise markets ... Here's an illustration from Olivier De Schutter and Jose Luis Vivero-Pol's work[2] around a 'tri-centric governance model' for food systems. For a radical and systemic transformation of the food economy, their thinking is that as well as the network of food enterprises we also need to think about and develop the so-called 'partner state' and 'the commons' where there is encouragement to provide appropriate infrastructure that focuses on tools for access, adding and distributing value and creating suitable markets, whether for non-profits or for profit. This does look like a promising theoretical model. It explores governance, private enterprise and the commons as three nested real world systems that can interact to enable new options and solutions for the food system.

In many countries civic collective actions for food are already happening with people producing food by themselves or getting organised in food buying groups, community supported agriculture or sharing meals clubs. The fast-growing constituency involved in this transition can value food as a commons. It calls for a different kind of state, the 'partner state', with different duties and skills to steer the transition. Olivier De Schutter and Jose Luis Vivero-Pol argue that these new functions are shaped by partnering and innovation rather than command-and-control via policies, subsidies, regulations and the use of force. A 'partner state' plays a role as shaper and creator of markets and facilitator for local people to engage with their local food commons e.g. land, food processing infrastructure. For the 'partner state', the priority is to prevent the enclosure of commons, as well as trigger the development and construction of new food commons. The 'partner state' oversees rules, cares for the commons (as mediator or judge) and is initiator of enabling legal frameworks for commoners to govern their commons.[2] This 'partner state' meanwhile also has characteristics of Mariana Mazzucato's so-called 'entrepreneurial state'[3]: it nurtures and finances social and technological innovations

Figure 30 (opposite page): A tri-centric governance model for food system transformation

Adapted from: Olivier De Schutter and Jose Luis Vivero-Po[2]

Illustration: Graham Pritchard

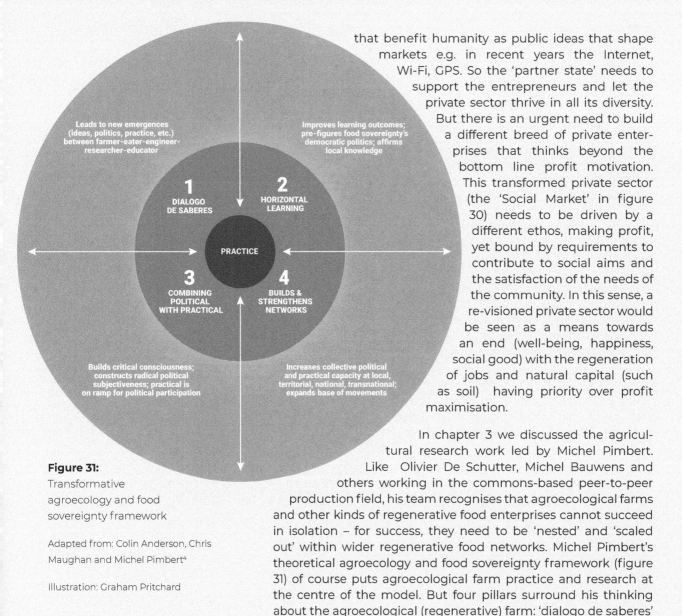

Leads to new emergences
(ideas, politics, practice, etc.)
between farmer-eater-engineer-
researcher-educator

Improves learning outcomes;
pre-figures food sovereignty's
democratic politics; affirms
local knowledge

1
DIALOGO
DE SABERES

2
HORIZONTAL
LEARNING

PRACTICE

3
COMBINING
POLITICAL
WITH PRACTICAL

4
BUILDS &
STRENGTHENS
NETWORKS

Builds critical consciousness;
constructs radical political
subjectiveness; practical is
on ramp for political participation

Increases collective political
and practical capacity at local,
territorial, national, transnational;
expands base of movements

Figure 31:

Transformative
agroecology and food
sovereignty framework

Adapted from: Colin Anderson, Chris
Maughan and Michel Pimbert[4]

Illustration: Graham Pritchard

that benefit humanity as public ideas that shape markets e.g. in recent years the Internet, Wi-Fi, GPS. So the 'partner state' needs to support the entrepreneurs and let the private sector thrive in all its diversity. But there is an urgent need to build a different breed of private enterprises that thinks beyond the bottom line profit motivation. This transformed private sector (the 'Social Market' in figure 30) needs to be driven by a different ethos, making profit, yet bound by requirements to contribute to social aims and the satisfaction of the needs of the community. In this sense, a re-visioned private sector would be seen as a means towards an end (well-being, happiness, social good) with the regeneration of jobs and natural capital (such as soil) having priority over profit maximisation.

In chapter 3 we discussed the agricultural research work led by Michel Pimbert. Like Olivier De Schutter, Michel Bauwens and others working in the commons-based peer-to-peer production field, his team recognises that agroecological farms and other kinds of regenerative food enterprises cannot succeed in isolation – for success, they need to be 'nested' and 'scaled out' within wider regenerative food networks. Michel Pimbert's theoretical agroecology and food sovereignty framework (figure 31) of course puts agroecological farm practice and research at the centre of the model. But four pillars surround his thinking about the agroecological (regenerative) farm: 'dialogo de saberes' (translated as 'wisdom dialogues' or roughly the equivalent of

Figure 32: Silerygaon village and farmland, Sikkim, India. In 2016, following a series of top-down policies and pesticide/fertilizer prohibitions, the state certified all agricultural production as organic by international standards. Coventry and Oregon Universities are currently working with the Sikkim government and farmers on the scale and food sovereignty politics of agroecological food systems[4]

Photo credit: Rudra Narayan Mitra

dialogue between ways of knowing); horizontal 'farmer to farmer' learning; political participation; and network building.[4] These four pillars (purple segments in figure 31) provide the living 'connective tissue' between systemic farm-level practice and the wider political project of food sovereignty nested in a transformed food system (orange circle).

Of course, in a devolved and distributed food network many participants do not have reserves of financial capital to invest but often they do have social capital and understand their locality well. Maybe it's also valuable to recognise the idea that, in systems terms, a thriving network of enterprises is not primarily about a 'tiddler' pool out of which some winners will be propelled to large-scale through a buy up (i.e. fulfilling the stereotype of an efficient to scale business, while the rest are failures). Rather, it is about a network of food enterprises which provide a thriving base, adding value to what is already available, that is able to *scale out* (rather than *scale up*) by propagation and replication, each network adjusted to local circumstances. These small and medium sized enterprises are often unable to draw down commercial capital

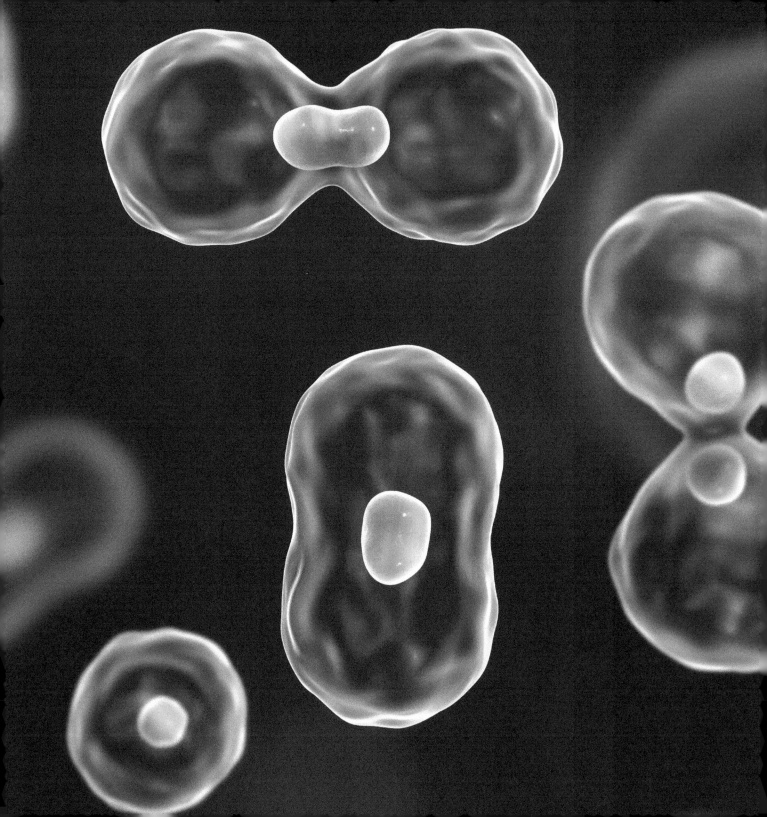

and need to resolve the chicken and egg challenges of having enough customers to thrive while large scale business extracts value from the region. To thrive, these smaller businesses need to see key public and private institutions circulating spending within their reach – perhaps regional or community banks, access to universal basic dividend, infrastructure and tools from which to build (see chapter 1).

The switch in focus needs to be away from how do these small scale, regenerative food and farming enterprises fit the norms of the globalised economy to how do we design new norms of governance where such enterprise is able to compete without structural disadvantage. These new norms are described under a number of headings such as the 'partner state', as already discussed, a revival of mutualism and cooperative ventures that encompasses emerging ideas around so-called 'open cooperatives' or after examples like the Preston Model in the UK[29], or as the 'foundational economy', that economy of essentials without which any economy fails. The parallel with the resilient, *exchange*-based features and processes of living organisms (e.g. blood circulation) or ecosystems is instructive, since this is where the bulk of the economic action always resides – as long as the idea of economy can escape the narrowly bounded and rather strange notion of it being just a singularly monetary phenomenon.

Cooperation often thrives in these small scale enterprise ecosystems – but it is also a highly competitive environment and will always remain so and the turnover of enterprises will reflect that: innovation and adaptation thrives. Contrast this with the situation where a few firms dominate – a situation that is typically characterised by the earning of economic rents and the rise in overall economic inefficiency due to this rent extraction (unearned income based on the creation or use of scarcity). A transformative circular economy is intuitively about circulating income not diverting it into an asset-based cycle with non-productive or 'parasitic' characteristics (see 'the monetary cycle' in chapter 1). As economist Jon Kay wrote: "almost all the strength of modern market economies is based on directing entrepreneurial activity from rent seeking into wealth creation".

This idea of a devolved, 'partner state' coupled with the aspirations of the new entrepreneurs seeking meaningful life choices is to make just the sort of redirection admired by Jon Kay but based on the recognition of the need for and opportunities in a systemic

Figure 33 (opposite page): Like dividing cells in the body, food enterprises need to scale out into a network by propagation and replication. Cell growth is nourished by surrounding nutrients from the blood – likewise, small enterprises are nurtured by the circulation of spending in the local economy

understanding of an effective system. If there were flags marking out the direction we might take a circular economy, it may be in this progression from *effective systems as a foundation to new wealth creation and participatory democracy* – not just voting every few years. We need a reinvigorated democracy (chapter 7) which comes from having a stake in society – something to lose and something to gain, knowing what to point towards. It may be about a collective sense of a better society reimagined beyond the conventional market-state duopoly, and building new kinds of business enterprises that use resources effectively at the same time as building the natural, social and economic capitals. *It is all about a systemic rebalancing, an evolution of, not a substitute for, the economy we have today.*

In the circular economy arena, it's become clear there is urgent need to work with insights from living systems to create natural capital rebuilding associated with more productive flows, to design material/energy cascades that utilise entrepreneurial initiative and to add value to what is already available. To date, such work is most often associated with Gunter Pauli and his publications *Plan A for Argentina*[5] and *The Third Dimension*[6], both with Juriaan Kamp and the *Blue Economy 3.0*[7]. Regrettably, Pauli's pioneering and successful work has often been ignored by a mainstream that focuses on a large scale and resource efficiency-based circular economy which is, at best, only a partial approach.

However, there's a need for further practical first-hand exploration of the kinds of systemic inputs, processes and enabling conditions necessary to successfully build a circular economy enterprise network that fits within the narrative framework discussed in this book.

Pauli's argument is that we need to get away from 2-D farming and shift to 3-D farming systems and networks. We need to think beyond industrialised 2-D monocultures like wheat spreading over vast agricultural landscapes with their shallow roots in a shallow and degrading soil layer. Instead, we need to move to the design of diverse 3-D polycultural farming systems that mimic the complex structures and processes found *above and below ground* (!) in natural ecosystems like forests and grasslands. To start to see the benefits of such rethinking let's pause to think about 3-D apple orchards...

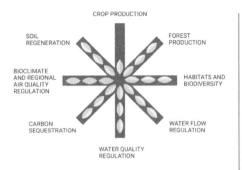

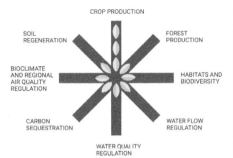

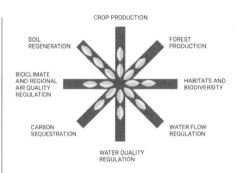

NATURAL APPLE FOREST

2D APPLE ORCHARD

EFFICIENCY OF CROP PRODUCTION
SYSTEM EMPHASISED

3D APPLE ORCHARD

EFFECTIVENESS OF CROP PRODUCTION
SYSTEM EMPHASISED

Figure 34 illustrates how a regenerative apple orchard mimics the structure and processes found in natural apple forests. Using a biomimetic design approach, the farmer aims to learn from the natural forest's 3-D vegetation and soil structure, nutrient and water cycles, energy flows, biodiversity, and interactions between species (such as cooperation, competition, symbiosis). Notice how, in contrast to the 2-D apple orchard shown in the illustration, there are high levels of carbon 'drawdown' (sequestration) in the structurally-diverse native apple forest and the 3-D apple orchard – in both, large quantities of carbon dioxide from the atmosphere are drawn down into the leaves through the process of photosynthesis, converted into carbon-based sugars and then eventually fixed in the soil as carbon/organic matter.

Figure 34: Regenerative apple orchards: from 2-D to 3-D design

Adapted from: US Department of Agriculture/ EPA[28]

Illustration: Graham Pritchard

Figure 35 (opposite page):

3-D ocean farm

Adapted from: Bren Smith[8]

Illustration: Graham Pritchard

Effectiveness means looking at the system not just a part of it.... A thought on effective versus efficient apple orchards: the *efficient* production of apples in an orchard is one which maximises yield/hectare of a suitable quality, produced with the minimum of inputs while preserving the viability of the apple crop for subsequent years. The efficient 2-D apple orchard (centre of figure 34) by defining itself narrowly, has always involved costs which are not borne by the producer – these are called the externalities. These include degrading soil structure, loss of biodiversity, pesticide and fertiliser run-off, and risk of short term crop viability (due to the monoculture emphasis). The loop is not closed in any meaningful sense, as capital is degraded and the wastes which are generated are not recovered/converted to assets. By contrast, an *effective* 3-D apple orchard is, by definition, one where capital is rebuilt and the overall resilience and durability of the system is accompanied by other potential benefits – additional biodiversity and cash flows (from other inter-planted crops and/or domestic livestock grazing in the orchard for instance). The overall (i.e. broadly described) productivity of an *effective* apple production system thus increases and the requirements of inputs are reduced. Of course, the higher productivity of biomass in this system does not equate to higher revenue if these biological material flows cannot be monetarised. The notion of 'system design' takes its place at this point. Although the design of effective and profitable systems is a challenge, the process is one which helps reinvent the idea of production in the 3-D apple orchard[30].

But the design of 3-D farming systems needs to move beyond terrestrial ecosystems – how about the oceans? That takes us right towards Bren Smith's innovative work with 3-D ocean farms off the east coast of the United States. His book *Eat Like a Fish*[8] reveals how his thinking is way beyond the monocultural 2-D offshore fishing that is so often dependent on the harvesting of a single species of high value fish, lobster or crab. His 3-D ocean farms mimic the complex structure and processes of coastal marine ecosystems. With echoes of George Chan and Mae Wan Ho's *Dream Farm 2.0*, his focus is on enterprise stacking around harvests from different components of the 3-D marine ecosystem, with a special emphasis on income generation opportunities with the different species of seaweed (kelp) that grow offshore. There are lessons to learn

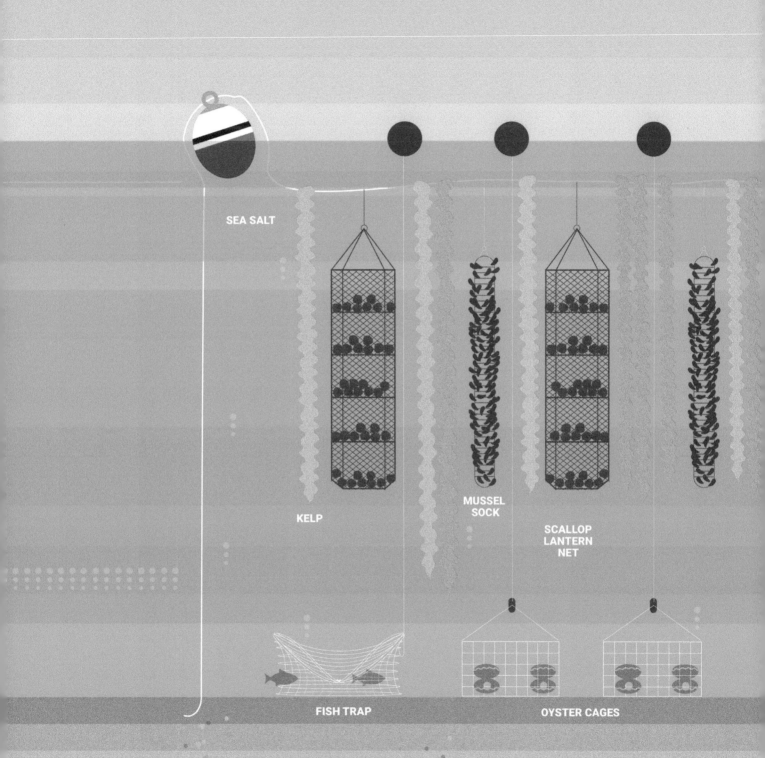

SEA SALT

KELP

MUSSEL
SOCK

SCALLOP
LANTERN
NET

FISH TRAP

OYSTER CAGES

from Bren Smith's extensive experience working at farm-scale as well as embedding 3-D ocean farms within wider food networks. In partnership with East Coast universities, he has well advanced work on open source tools and learning programmes for the scaling out of 3-D ocean farms. Smith is clear on the need to scale out: "our vision for scale is building...'reefs', composed of 25-50 small-scale farms in a region and a processing hub and hatchery on land, encircled by a rink of entrepreneurs developing value added products. These reefs are then replicated up and down our coastlines. This allows for scaling through networks rather than massive, vertically integrated, industrial farms at sea."[8]

There is an urgent need for more research around these 3-D farming systems. The design approach for this research is to firstly to define what the interacting components are:

- Take an orchard or coastal fish farm and design biomimetic and regenerative '3-D approaches' – create enterprises with many biological nutrient flows, cash flows and benefits.
- Enable access to the commons: give farmers secure access and user rights on commons occuring on land and sea that is in both private and public ownership.
- Build some commons-based infrastructure: such as a community kitchen and temporary materials storage and a local transport asset (shared).
- Add some market stimulus via improved procurement opportunities for local food producers or loans for local micro enterprises.
- Address limited consumer demand for locally-sourced food from regenerative farms and horticultural enterprises - potentially by working with local government to pilot application of a localised universal basic dividend e.g. the RSA[9] recently recommended pilot work on a so-called 'Beetroot Bond' (see Box 3) (say £10/month/citizen for purchase of produce from local regenerative food enterprises).
- Encourage research and innovation (especially university/business partnerships) e.g. application of used biodegradable diapers as compost in the orchards[10] (see figure 40) or, say, plant genetics work on different species of seaweed.

What is innovative here is the deliberate use of 'new' land and sea-based commons and commons-based infrastructure or access to existing infrastructure, a happiness to countenance micro enterprises as learning platforms and incubators and a firm belief in building natural, social and financial capital – including soil regeneration. There's also focus on the importance of try-out, feedback and adaptation with a clear commitment to the involvement of universities, business, government and citizen organisations within the specific geographical region.

Some of the key research questions for future studies: in what circumstances could this small(er) scale production thrive in food networks so that it contributes to soil regeneration and better food (and diet) for all (or for a lot more)? How important is affordability? What if we could free up people's enterprising spirit, what would it take and what would then happen in the food enterprise network?

Other important research questions: how could such 3-D orchards and ocean farms fit and add value to established local food networks in a particular geographical region? How could these 3-D farming enterprises scope out within and add resilience and effectiveness to wider food enterprise networks (those economies of scope again)?

BOX 3

'THE BEETROOT BOND'

"A universal community bond proposes a bold approach to tackling the problems we face in the food system, giving everyone a real and practical incentive to participate in and shape a sustainable food system in their communities...It is an idea as radical and transformational – and in the same vein – as universal basic income.

Every person in the UK, adult and child, would receive a Beetroot Bond with a monthly dividend to spend on fresh food. The purpose is to nudge people to buy healthy food and to empower communities to shape and drive their local food systems. The money would only be available to spend on healthy produce purchased directly from local farmers and traders. It would ultimately be the decision for the local community, through a community food plan within a national framework, to determine which businesses and initiatives are eligible. They could include, for example, local and seasonal, organic or other high welfare accreditations, plastic-free, fairly traded or affordable. This would enable everyone to access good food, and recognise that this is fundamental to our personal health and wellbeing as well as that of our communities. The Beetroot Bonds would also be shares in your local food system. Each person would be able to use their Beetroot 'shares' (and the shares of their dependents) to vote on local food policy. Through a digital democracy platform all 'shareholders' would be able to vote on how (within the nationally defined framework) Beetroot Pounds can be spent in their community....".

Source: *Our Future in the Land. Food,* Farming and Countryside Commission. RSA. (2019)[9]

**PANARCHY AND ADAPTIVE CYCLES -
COMPLEX SYSTEMS NATURALLY GROW,
BECOME MORE BRITTLE, COLLAPSE,
AND THEN RENEW THEMSELVES IN AN
ENDLESS CYCLE**

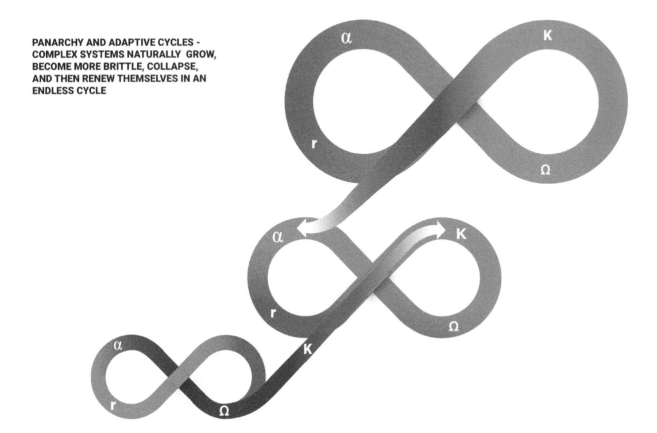

REORGANISATION PHASE
A time of innovation,
restructuring and greatest
uncertainty but with
high resilience.

GROWTH PHASE
Is characterised by: rapid
accumulation of resources
(capitals), competition, seizing
of opportunities, rising level of
diversity and connections, and
high but decreasing, reslience.

CONSERVATION PHASE
Growth slows down as resources
are stored and used largely for
system maintenance. This phase
is characterised by: stability,
certainty, reduced flexibility,
and low resilience.

CREATIVE DESTRUCTION PHASE
This phase is characterised by
chaotic collapse and release of
accumulated capital. This is a
time of uncertainty when
resilience is low but increasing.

We're inspired by one of the U.K.'s leading local food networks – Tamar Grow Local – a community interest company (CIC), based on the Devon and Cornwall border of south-west England. Managed by Simon Platten, this CIC supports a network of over 90 food enterprises and uses the internationally respected Open Food Network open-source software[11] to market their local and seasonal food produce. Platten[12] has a sound grasp of complex systems theory as well as its practical application in the Tamar Grow Local food network:

"(the figures 36 and 37 over page) illustrate the way in which adaptive cycles of different scales can link with, and impact upon, each other. Tamar Grow Local has borrowed rather literally from the (panarchy) heuristic and structured their work on a similar three tier model. The second tier projects such as the food hub and the produce co-ops, are at a different scale to those (tier 1 food producers) that make use of them. They also safe-guard the elements that the first tier community initiatives make use of. When an un-networked community initiative or business comes to the end of its lifespan its system fragments. This can result in resources being lost including assets such as equipment and land, and the key people involved (with their associated knowledge). Most assets within Tamar Grow Local, however, are embedded at the second tier level, and in turn are held by Tamar Grow Local CIC which has an asset lock. To borrow from social and ecological systems vocabulary, the second tier projects (and Tamar Grow Local CIC more generally) 'remember' for those acting at a smaller (faster) scale and are able to steer their 'release' and 'reorganisation' phases..."

In this way, Simon Platten and colleagues argue[12] that if a food production/growing initiative in tier 1 ends, its resources can be readily cycled into a new business enterprise within the same niche, thereby continuing the purpose and objectives of the larger scale food system. So, metaphorically at least, new trees are planted (enterprises) and the Tamar Grow Local woodland maintained (the wider Tamar Valley food network). The first tier initiatives hold much of the adaptive capacity within the Tamar

Figure 36 (opposite page): Panarchy and adaptive cycles

Adapted from: Buzz Holling[13]

Illustration: Graham Pritchard

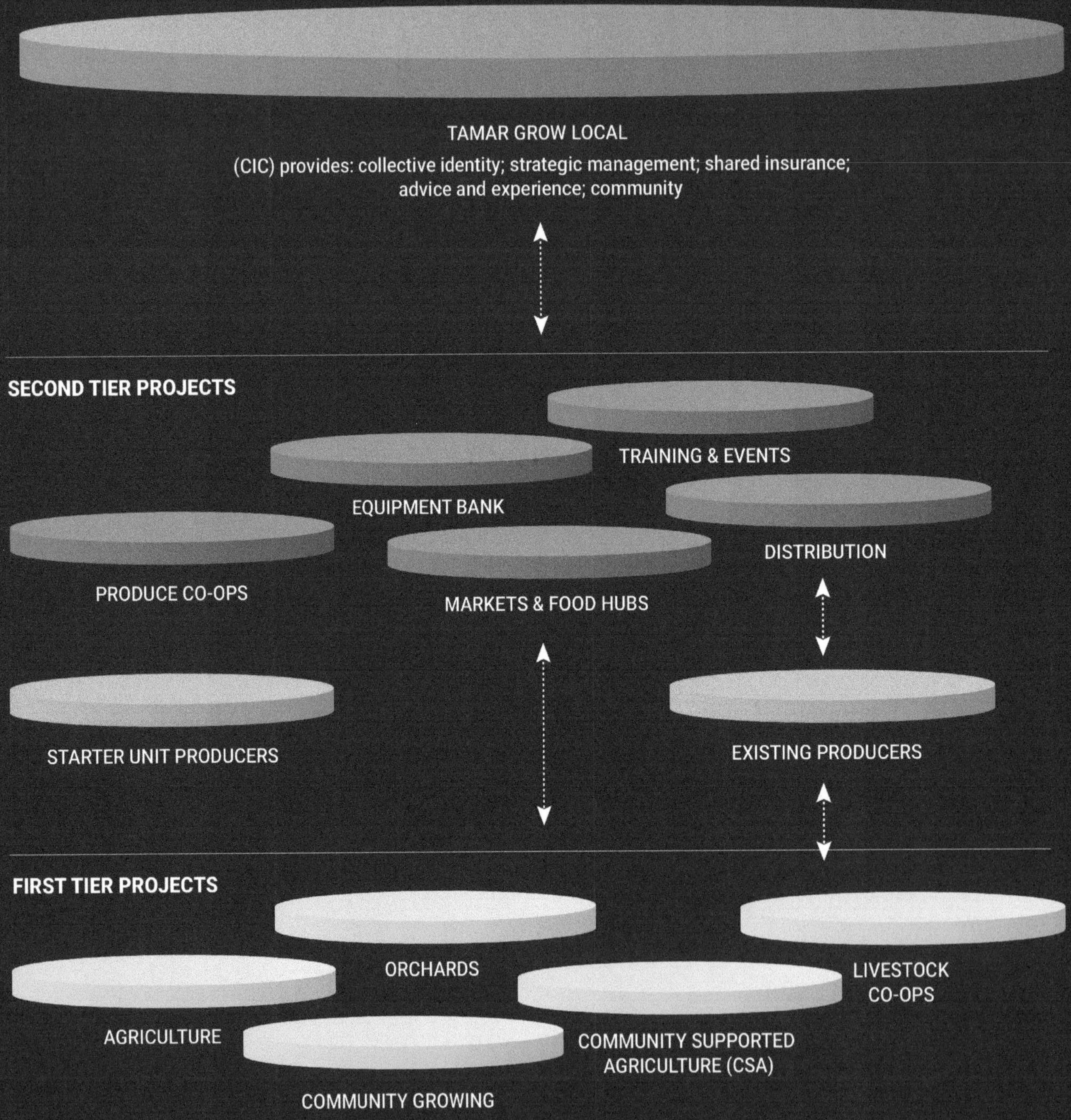

TAMAR GROW LOCAL

(CIC) provides: collective identity; strategic management; shared insurance; advice and experience; community

SECOND TIER PROJECTS

TRAINING & EVENTS

EQUIPMENT BANK

DISTRIBUTION

PRODUCE CO-OPS

MARKETS & FOOD HUBS

STARTER UNIT PRODUCERS

EXISTING PRODUCERS

FIRST TIER PROJECTS

ORCHARDS

LIVESTOCK CO-OPS

AGRICULTURE

COMMUNITY SUPPORTED AGRICULTURE (CSA)

COMMUNITY GROWING

Grow Local model. There is a certain degree of 'churn' within first tier initiatives that is important for the resilience of a system as a whole, as this is one way in which new approaches and new models (for example, say 3-D orchards and ocean farms) might emerge to add value and become incorporated into the wider adaptive food system.

The authors are currently working with partners in Kyrgyzstan on the development of a research proposal for a 'Dream Farm'/3-D apple orchard network in the Tien Shan Mountains of Central Asia. Why Kyrgyzstan as the choice for a research study area?

First, quite literally, this part of the world is the cradle of apple evolution. The Tien Shan Mountains' native apple forests are home to the ancestors of the domestic apple varieties that are now cultivated throughout the temperate regions of the world. On the slopes of the Tien Shan mountain range lie the scattered remnants of a vast ancient forest that was home to many of the species that would give rise to the fruits and nuts accompanying humans throughout their history (apples but also plums, apricots, walnuts and pistachio). Wild apple forests still stretch across many parts of these mountains which are up to 7,000 metres high, with deep valleys carved out by over 200 rivers, plateaus and slopes with different orientations leading to vast differences in temperature and humidity. Because of this landscape diversity in the Tien Shan there is an extraordinary diversity of apple tree species and varieties that persists today despite thousands of years of deforestation and fires to clear land for farming. This apple tree diversity expresses itself in fruits of many different shapes, sizes, flavours, and colours, and in trees with differing heights and habits. It represents a genetic pool of immeasurable interest for research that could be key to the future of apple cultivation[14]. There is so much potential to feature and celebrate the Tien Shan mountains apple tree diversity in a 3-D apple orchard research programme. A 'what we learned in the apple forest' field trip in the recently established

Figure 37 (opposite): Tamar Grow Local food network

Adapted from: Simon Platten[12]

Illustration: Graham Pritchard

Figure 38: Native apple forest in autumn. Tien Shan Mountains, Central Asia

Photo credit: Sergey Dyonin

Western Tien Shan Mountains World Heritage Site[15] will be a likely priority for the research team. Time spent in the apple forests of these mountains should produce a bountiful yield of design ideas for the structure and apple variety make-up of future 3-D apple orchards!

Secondly, a research programme in Kyrgyzstan provides an exciting opportunity to retell the apple origin story and the wealth of myths and legends about apples found in so many cultures of the world. Because of its value as a food crop, it was from here in Central Asia that apples were transported along the Silk Road trading networks (figure 39). Stretching east to China, stretching west to Europe and North America, apple cultivation and orchards flourished. It was the ancient Chinese, Greeks and Romans who pioneered the art of apple tree 'grafting'. European settlers carried the apples and their pips for their orchards in America[16] and in China farmers perfected the breeding to produce the unique softer, sweeter fruits of Chinese dessert apples[17]. Together, wild and domesticated animals (bears and horses with apple pips in their dung) and humans participated in a giant genetic laboratory that led to the diffusion of the apple and its subsequent domestication.

In their beautiful book *The wild apple forests of the Tien Shan*, Catherine Peix and Natalya Ogar[18] document the emergence of apple cultivation in the Tien Shan Mountains and how this valuable food crop then laid the foundations for human cultures expressed in myths, symbols, cultivations, landscapes and cuisines, and now an irreplaceable heritage of biodiversity for people around the world. Symbol of fertility, immortality, love and beauty, wealth and power, knowledge and damnation, the apple has been identified as the fruit that Eve tempted Adam with, the fruit 'sweet to [the] palate' in the Song of Solomon, the golden apple of the Hesperides, of the Celtic myth of Avalon, and the fruit whose fall inspired Isaac Newton to define the law of gravity[18]. So the apple is not just a symbol of our food and farming systems and orchards. Through story and legend we can also see how the apple is an important symbol of human culture, knowledge, insight and expertise.

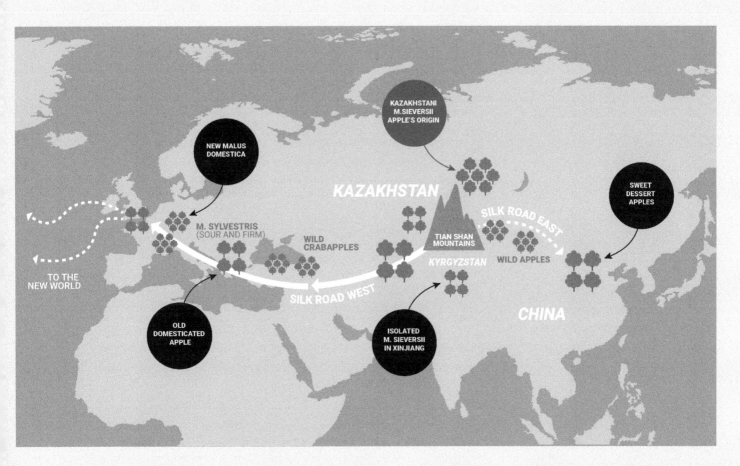

Figure 39: Origin of domesticated apple: dispersal along Silk Road trade networks

Adapted from: Nicola Davis[17]

Illustration: Graham Pritchard

Another reason for the choice of Kyrgyzstan as a 3-D apple orchard study area: this region has such a rich history and thriving tradition in apple cultivation. Evgeniya Postnova from AKMENA, based in Bishkek, Kyrgyzstan reports[19] on the importance of commercial apple cultivation for Kyrgyzstan, with, on average, 140,000 tonnes of apples grown per year. In some provinces of the country (especially in Chui, Issyk-Kul and Osh provinces) about 40% of the population of rural areas is engaged in apple culti-vation. Most apples are grown by individual farmers - nowadays there are no big state apple orchards, as under the Soviet Union.

Postnova believes this is a timely opportunity to establish regenerative farming and horticulture approaches in Kyrgyzstan's apple sector - many of the small-scale farmers are sympathetic to these approaches, already utilising their orchards for beekeeping and to harvest hay for cattle and for foraging by chickens. She urges[20] Kyrgyzstan farmers to end "the focusing down on the apple, even if it is a better, more suitable cultivar. Instead, focusing up is to find the forest and think what might be the biggest number of benefits we can find from a 'forest orchard', one which uses the many layers and varieties of an apple-walnut forest i.e. multiple cash flows, more from less land - and all the biodiversity too. This is adding value to what we already have, by designing an ecosystem of business to go alongside the ecosystem of species - it means much more than apples of course and it demands a systems thinking which traditional farmers have always known – but brought up to date."

The Kyrgyz Government has recently established new apple harvest logistics centres and the country's first online market for apples. An important research question: how could future 3-D apple orchards scope out and add resilience and effectiveness to these apple logistics centres, online market and wider food enterprise networks in Kyrgyzstan?

The apple is, in its industrial, efficient form in Kyrgyzstan and in many other parts of the world, so narrowly conceived that nowadays only a very few varieties dominate our shops because they are seen as the best ones to suit the mechanics of growing, picking and packing in the 21st century. Currently, the apple is an example of underused abundance, with wasteful and narrowly conceived production and neglected by-products and additional cash flows – just because that's what producers are told the market demands. Set the enabling economic conditions right though and the specialist apple cultivar, or the large apple tree root stock, is not just the latest food fad of the already well off, or an apple tree too big to manage – instead, these cultivars and rootstocks could underpin important research programmes and exciting new social and economic possibilities based around production, exchange and regeneration of natural capital.

What could this start to look like in small-scale 3-D apple orchards? What about community-building aspects of apple orchards? There's a long history of customs and games that we have created around the apple and these echo the importance it has had in peoples lives (see box 4). Traditional customs should, of course, still be at the heart of our apple orchards going forward. But what about innovation and new approaches for community-building based around the apple orchard? Just one idea from Berlin, Germany: DYCLE is aiming to be one of the world's first fully zero-waste, companies for baby diapers. DYCLE is building communities around parents and babies, offering a 100% bio-based, and 100% compostable, diaper inlay. The inlays are collected within the community and transformed into high quality compost for soil regeneration which then supports the growth of newly planted fruit and nut tree orchards. Currently, small clusters of families are researching and learning about the feasibility of 'diaper cycle fruit orchards' in Berlin. But in future the plan is to create distributed networks of diaper producers and orchards in and around other towns and cities - each using their own source of diapers as material inputs for compost production. Gunter Pauli is involved with DCYCLE as an ambassador and his 'double digit growth model'[21] is at the heart of the project: "respond to basic needs with local products and services". This is about innovation and adding value at all levels: from diaper production; to the composting; to the relationships with parents and babies; to the regeneration of healthy soil. The community-based research team in Berlin is breaking

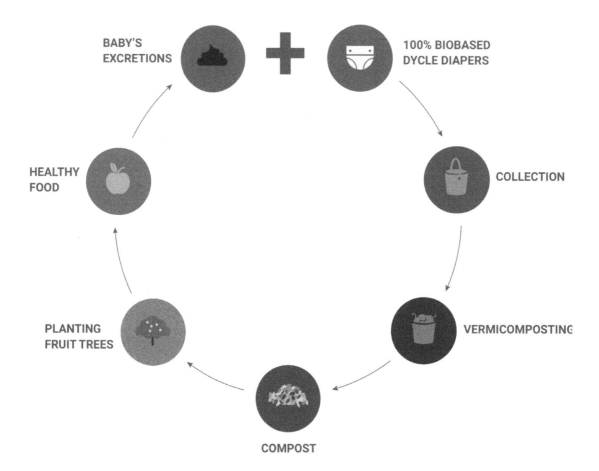

Figure 40: The diaper cycle in a community fruit orchard

Adapted from: DYCLE[22]

Ilustration: Graham Pritchard

new ground by exploring the development of a value chain with multiple income streams that produce high quality regenerative products, at competitive prices, whilst building social capital and community along the way. Apples, plums, cherries and other fruits harvested from the trees could be procured for baby food and juice production, thus closing the nutrients (urine/faeces) cycle of baby diapers. DYCLE estimates that 1,000 kg of compost can be produced from one year's supply of diapers from a single child[22]. Waste=food for sure.

Some thoughts on systemic health

If the focus needs to be on action research, learning and feedback in food enterprise networks we should probably try to get to grips with some measures of 'systemic health'... For that, let's turn to John Fullerton, an ex-financier and President of the Capital Institute. He included this slide from Sally Goerner (figure 41) in a recent talk. It tries to show some starting points for guaging systemic health. It draws on the 'regenerative economies' idea, like much circular economy discussion, but unpacking the diagram gives a few more clues. It's based on insights from living systems so it has a nested system feel. The illustration hints at the notion of related scales both visually alongside the measure of 'cross-scale circulation' (spot the fractal, the branching system) and in the way flows operate in such a system through 'the balance of resilience and efficiency'.

There are the expected input and output characteristics 'reliable' and 'healthy', coupled with that key function of capital building ('regenerative re-investments'). This is not about 'let's-capture-the-flow pipework'. Other measures of note in figure 41 are the systems 'diversity', 'balance of sizes' and 'constructive versus extractive' activity. Goerner[24] identifies a need to assess the balance between overly extractive and speculative processes and more constructive activities that build economic, social and environmental capitals e.g. infrastructure and learning.

> ## BOX 2
> ### APPLE CUSTOMS AND GAMES – SOME EXAMPLES FROM ENGLAND
>
> *"...almost every farm and big garden used to have its own orchard of mixed fruit trees for domestic use and farm labourers were often part paid in cider... City folk travelled to pick fruit in the (countryside)... Costermongers (apple sellers) cries rang out in street markets, and greengrocers put out baths of water for games of 'duck apple' at Halloween, known as Dookie Apple Night in Newcastle and Duck Apple Night in Liverpool. In Mobberley, Cheshire and other places, 'crabbing the parson' was practised, crabapples pelted at the vicar on the local saints day. Griggling, a'scraggling, souling, pothering and ponking, a'cattin, going a gooding, clemening, worsting, howling and youling and taking round the calennig are just some of the local traditions.*
>
> *It takes time for customs to differentiate themselves, just as an intricate landscape demonstrates the deep relationship that we and nature have developed over hundreds of years. The rich repertoire of apple games and customs links season, produce and locality, yet we are in danger of forgetting what they mean because we have ceased to value our apples and orchards..."*
>
> **Source:** *England in Particular.* Clifford, S. and King, A. Common Ground. (2006)[23]

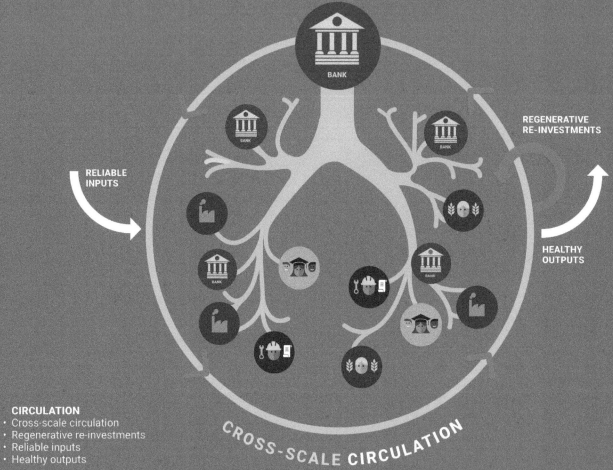

RELIABLE
INPUTS

REGENERATIVE
RE-INVESTMENTS

HEALTHY
OUTPUTS

BANK

CROSS-SCALE CIRCULATION

CIRCULATION
· Cross-scale circulation
· Regenerative re-investments
· Reliable inputs
· Healthy outputs

STRUCTURE
· Balance of sizes
· Balance of resilience & efficiency
· Sufficient number & diversity of roles

RELATIONSHIPS & VALUES
· Degree of mutualism
· Constructive vs extractive

COLLECTIVE LEARNING
· Collective learning

In short, the diagram features insights from a framework for thinking which is derived from the rules, processes and structures of complex adaptive systems. But the very terms implied in this diagram – fractal, allometric scaling, diversity and resilience for example – and the difficulty of imagining what applying this kind of framework means in practice severely dampens down progress. It's actually a theory-practice gap *where what's missing is the theory*! It's not as if we are missing the practice and examples because of some lack of will or opportunity – what we are missing is a framework for thinking. Einstein's observation "the theory determines what is observed", as an expression of insights from complex adaptive systems, is ground zero for the circular economy. Yet currently most circular economy practice in contrast is developing and reflecting on the system as 'pipework' where technical and biological material leaks need fixing and rebuilding capital is just a nice-to-have. The very language of such practice is littered with machine metaphors – 'building blocks', 'drivers', 'levers' and 'efficiency' rather than 'effectiveness' – where it often feels like Bill Mcdonough's and Michael Braungart's cradle to cradle principle 'celebrate diversity' is ignored or just given lip service. We need to recognise that diversity in economic systems, just like in culture and natural ecosystems, is a means to resilience and creativity; diversity is a system condition for the evolution of economies. This one example shines a light on the paucity of insight in much of the current thinking about the circular economy.

A few concluding observations on how to scale out regenerative food enterprise networks...we need to be clear about what we understand by the terms 'scaling up' and 'scaling out' – and what we mean by the 'ecology' of regenerative farming businesses. For us, successful scaling out of regenerative agriculture is about the development of distributed local and regional food networks... food networks that are complex, dynamic and living

Figure 41 (opposite page): Measures of systemic health. The healthy system is nourished by cross-scale circulation of materials, money, information and energy

Adapted from: Sally Goerner/RARE/Capital Institute[24]

Illustration: Graham Pritchard

systems...with individual regenerative farms and market gardens nested within distributed local and regional food networks, and with those food networks nested within a wider transformed food system. For success at local and regional geographic scales, we need to be thinking about food producers (different sizes, different – 'polycultural'[25] – business types etc.), land (varying land usership/ownership/access models, including the 'commons' etc.) and food consumers connected in distributed (rather than/as well as centralised) food networks/ecosystems. Food and energy stocks and flows, monetary value creation and distribution, soil regeneration and social capital building all need to be factored in if we want to achieve systemically-healthy food networks.

In answer to that question "how can we 'scale out' regenerative agriculture?" Sally Goerner argues[26] that the only way such food and farming enterprises will compete with large-scale monoculture industrial farming is by banding together in more synergistic and more effective 'learning food networks'. Quoting her: "it's not how big you grow as a business, it's how you grow big". For her, the goal is not to stay small so much as to use distributed ownership to counter oligarchic trends orientated to the privileged few.

For success, we need to start to visualise distributed food networks in relation to the sort of measures she details in figure 41. When thinking about robust cross-scale circulation, exchange and regenerative return flows, as well as healthy food flows (and diets), we need to address soil regeneration (it's so much about critical natural capital). An important indicator of a successful scaled-out regional food network would be when accumulating stocks of food 'waste' in urban areas start to get composted at scale to enable regenerative return flows of (non-polluted) biological nutrients and organic matter (compost) to the soil in urban and peri-urban settings. Another indicator of a healthy regional food network might be evidence of the seeding and growth of diverse food enterprises, beyond just growing food e.g. use of food and agricultural waste as feedstocks for the emerging bioplastics economy.

Jose Luis Vivero Pol's governance model for food systems (figure 30) gives us a final reminder of the possible role of 'partner state' government in this growth of regenerative food enterprise networks...the government has to be able and willing to help to create a loosely coupled, decentralised and distributed food system infrastructure, and then wait. Waiting means observing how providing this infrastructure affects the coupling – the feed-back – and then adjusting accordingly. It speaks of evolution – try-out, learn and adapt (including perhaps with a local currency and credit focus). The role does not mean engineering food system solutions for people and business enterprises. Instead, it means to take on 'wise governance'... it means keeping a careful eye on the measures and tell-tale signs of a healthy mix between govern-ment activity, autonomous civil society/commons food initiatives and a transformed private sector – making profit yet bound by requirements to contribute to social aims and the wider needs of surrounding communities.

One final point: we need to remember that small scale food enterprise networks are by nature highly competitive – the high turnover of enterprises means that innovation and adaptation thrives in the ecosystem. Yet cooperation can and should also flourish both within and across these enterprise networks. They need to mimic those forest ecosystems where both cooperation and competition are in play together. Recent research in the giant redwood forests of British Columbia, Canada[27] has revealed important new insights on this cooperation-competition dynamic in natural ecosystems. Forest ecologist Suzanne Simard has used radiocarbon-tagged nutrients in the trees and soils to reveal how trees of different species cooperate by sharing and exchanging nutrients from the soil – this nutrient exchange takes place over large areas of forest floor thanks to the soil fungal networks that link up the trees and tree roots covering large patches of forest – the so-called 'wood wide web'. Food enterprise networks need to mimic this wood wide web.

Chapter references and notes

1. Ploeg, van der, J.D., Jingzhong, Y. and Schneider, S. (2012). Rural development through the construction of new, nested, markets: comparative perspectives from China, Brazil and the European Union. *Journal of Peasant Studies* 39

https://www.researchgate.net/publication/233337679_Rural_development_through_the_construction_of_new_nested_markets_comparative_perspectives_from_China_Brazil_and_the_European_Union

2. De Schutter, O., Mattei, U., Jose Luis Vivero-Pol, J. and Ferrando, T. (2019). Food as Commons: towards a new relationship between the public, the civic and the private. Chapter 24 in: *Routledge Handbook of Food Commons* (open access book chapter). Routledge.

https://www.routledge.com/Routledge-Handbook-of-Food-as-a-Commons-1st-Edition/Vivero-Pol-Ferrando-De-Schutter-Mattei/p/book/9781138062627

3. Mazzucato, M. *The Entrepreneurial State: Debunking Public vs. Private Sector Myths*. Anthem Press. (2013). Also see: Mazzucato, M. *Mission economy: a moonshot guide to changing capitalism*. Allen Lane. (2021)

4. Anderson, C., Maughan, C. and Pimbert, M. (2019) Transformative agro-ecology learning in Europe: building consciousness, skills and collective capacity for food sovereignty. *Agric Hum Values* 36, 531–547

https://link.springer.com/article/10.1007/s10460-018-9894-0#citeas

Coventry University agroecology research with Sikkim government and small scale farmers http://www.agroecologynow.com/projects/sikkim/

5. Pauli, G. and Kamp, J. *Plan A. The transformation of Argentina's economy*. JJK Books. (2017)

6. Pauli, G. and Kamp, J. *The Third Dimension. 3-D farming and 11 more unstoppable trends that are revolutionising the production of food and fuel, regenerating nature and rebuilding communities.* JJK Books. (2017)

7. Pauli, G. *The Blue Economy 3.0. The marriage of science, innovation and entrepreneurship create a new business model that transforms society.* Xlibris. (2017)

8. Smith, B. *Eat Like a Fish: My adventures as a fisherman turned restorative ocean farmer.* Murdoch Books. (2019)

9. *Our Future in the Land.* Food, Farming and Countryside Commission. RSA. (2019). Beetroot bond reference on page 26

https://www.thersa.org/discover/publications-and-articles/reports/future-land

10. Diaper cycle in fruit orchards. DYCLE https://dycle.org/en

11. Open Food Network https://www.openfoodnetwork.org/about-us/

Tamar Grow Local food hub https://www.tamarvalleyfoodhubs.org.uk/

12. Platten, S. *A local food system designed for resilience.* Tamar Grow Local CIC (2017).

https://sharedassets.org.uk/wp-content/uploads/2018/01/Tamar-Grow-Local-Case-Study.pdf

13. Gunderson, L. and Holling, C. *Panarchy: Understanding transformations in human and natural systems.* Edited by L. Gunderson and C. Holling. Island Press. (2002)

Good explanation of panarchy theory at the Resilience Alliance website https://www.resalliance.org/panarchy

14. *The wild apple forests of the Tien Shan.* Citation XXVII Annual Award, 2016

http://www.fbsr.it/wp-content/uploads/2016/03/English-text_Citation1.pdf

15. UNESCO World Heritage Site document on Western Tien Shan Mountains. (2016)

http://whc.unesco.org/uploads/nominations/1490.pdf

16. Huxley, A. *Green Inheritance*. Gaia Books. (1984)

17. Davis, N. (2017). Geneticists trace humble apple's exotic lineage all the way to the Silk Road. *The Guardian*

https://www.theguardian.com/science/2017/aug/15/geneticists-trace-humble-apples-exotic-lineage-all-the-way-to-the-silk-road

18. *The wild apple forests of the Tien Shan*. The International Carlo Scarpa Prize for Gardens 2016, XXVII edition. Edited by Giuseppe Barbera, Patrizia Boschiero, Luigi Latini, with Catherine Peix. Fondazione Benetton Studi Ricerche Treviso. (2016)

http://www.fbsr.it/en/publication/the-wild-apple-forests-of-the-tien-shan/

19. *Kyrgyzstan – apple orchards*. Ken Webster pers. comm. with Evgeniya Postnova from AKMENA. 2018

20. Postnova, E. (2018). Kyrgyzstan - the homeland of apples: from the beginnings to 21st century Renaissance. AKMENA

21. Pauli, G. *Blue Growth: Reflections on How to Get Out of The Poverty and Jobless Trap through a Bottom-Up Scenario*. Blog. (2015) http://www.gunterpauli.com/blog/blue-growth

22. DYCLE website https://dycle.org/en

23. Clifford, S. and King, A. *England in Particular*. Common Ground. Hodder & Stoughton. (2006)

Common Ground Apple Gazette for English counties https://www.commonground.org.uk/an-apples-orchards-gazetteer/

24. Fath, B., Fiscus, D., Goerner, S., Berea, A. and Ulanowicz, R. (2019). Measuring regenerative economics: 10 principles and measures undergirding systemic economic health. Global Transitions, 1, pp. 15-27

https://reader.elsevier.com/reader/sd/pii/S2589791819300040?token=69AFBF51355B5132D7BA0129ACA65130CB44D2A8C2D-922772E0674DE1E2815DE431608C72910D98433B654302I1E197A

25. Polycultural ownership models. Jolley, A. *The Co-op Farming Model Might Help Save America's Small Farms.* (2018)

https://civileats.com/2018/10/03/co-op-farming-models-might-help-save-americas-small-farms/amp/?__twitter_impression=true

Polycultural models: ... "the single-owner model... means relying on a 'monoculture of the mind,'..... we know it's important to have polyculture in our seeds and farming system, and in turn we also need that in terms of who's managing the farm."

26. Sally Goerner pers. comm. Craig Johnson. October 15, 2018

27. Beiler, K. and Simard, S. (2009). Architecture of the wood-wide web: Rhizopogon spp. genets link multiple Douglas-fir cohorts. *New Phytologist*, 185 pp. 543-5.

https://www.researchgate.net/publication/38056764_Architecture_of_the_wood-wide_web_Rhizopogon_spp_genets_link_multiple_Douglas-fir_cohorts3

28. EPA/US Department of Agriculture. *Enhancing Ecosystem Services from Agricultural Lands: Management, Quantification and Developing Decision Support Tools.* (2009)

https://cfpub.epa.gov/ncer_abstracts/index.cfm/fuseaction/display.rfatext/rfa_id/508

29. The Preston model https://www.preston.gov.uk/article/1339/What-Is-Preston-Model-

30. For an example of an organic arable farm system redesigned along 3-D orchard principles see: https://www.edp24.co.uk/business/farming/agroforesty-pioneer-stephen-briggs-at-agriteche-event-1-6812620

31. Mark Drewell is Executive Chairman of New Foundation Farms https://newfoundation.farm/#about

CHAPTER 5

CITIES IN A CIRCULAR ECONOMY
"In the long term, an economic rethink and reboot is needed".
Larry Elliot[24]

CLOSED

THE NEIGHBOURHOOD

EPARTMENT STORE IS
HOUSE OF FRASER

ANDECAY.CO.UK

What is it with cities? As they search for economic development can they create an economy which is regenerative, accessible and abundant, including food systems, and do it by intention or design?   Cities care about many things: affordable housing, decent jobs, economic development and community building are just the start. They also care about pollution, waste management, hygiene, and more – air pollution is one of the top health issues and a clear marker to whether a city is attractive, not only to its own citizens but to others. China may have been influenced by the reaction to the smogs threatening the Peking Olympics in its decision in 2018 to ban the import of waste plastics[1], much of which was being burnt.

Since a regenerative, inclusive circular economy can, in the right circumstances, contribute to the upside it might seem a little picky to qualify this with the question what *kind* of circular economy? Aren't they all the same? The reason it matters very much has something to do with these questions: are we headed for a new economic paradigm which recognises the interplay between efficiency and resilience and works on all scales? Or are we headed somewhere else entirely? (see figure 42)

Everyone and their dog want to claim the word 'paradigm' (and it's usual to be over dramatic with language these days). So let's ask, instead, but with a few added flourishes: are we headed towards an economy which is more devolved, and one where the main questions are not about production so much as access and distribution? If it is more devolved, who controls the distribution and of what? Then we will know where to locate food.

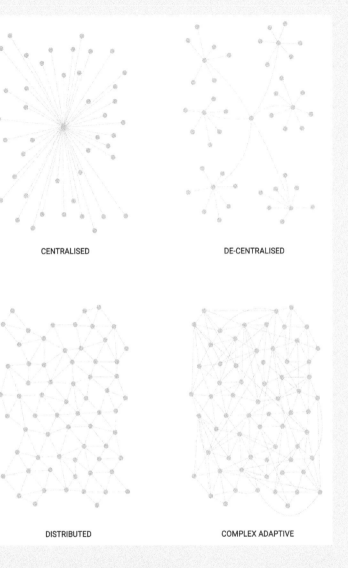

CENTRALISED

DE-CENTRALISED

DISTRIBUTED

COMPLEX ADAPTIVE

Figure 42: Are we headed for a new economic paradigm? Centralised, decentralised, distributed and complex adaptive systems

Adapted from: Paul Baran[2]

Illustration: Graham Pritchard

Archetypal system structures can be found in the illustration here (figure 42). They all exist in cities but to varying degrees. Christopher Alexander, an early systems guy and architect, wrote an article entitled *A City is Not a Tree*[3]. What he meant was that we incorrectly see cities as just following a treelike structure right down to the last alleyway and individual. He had observed that instead the centralised and decentralised structures led on to a 'semi-lattice', as he called it, something we would now call a distributed network. Citizens as citizens were more than mere consumers and were often producers too. Consumer, producer and citizen. This sounds like the 'civis', the root of the word civilisation. Hence a great deal of exchange, not all of it monetary by any means, occurred within the city. It still does, except now there are pressures in two directions. Firstly, the digital revolution has reduced the power of smaller scale retail and, in production and disintermediation, has left bigger businesses with power over the network of exchange and the production and sale (or access/use) of goods and services. In the other direction, writers like Doug Rushkoff see the internet, by contrast, as a disintermediation[23] technology to enable a more distributed peer-to-peer arrangement which would empower (as the saying goes) the individual and small group towards autonomy – the social production mentioned by Jeremy Rifkind, Paul Mason, and, of course, Michel Bauwens.

The systems scientist W. Brian Arthur raises another point in a recent McKinsey article[4]

"I will argue [technological change] is causing the economy to enter a new and different era. The economy has arrived at a point where it produces enough in principle for everyone, but where the means of access to these services, products and jobs, is steadily tightening. So this new period we are entering is not so much about production anymore – how much is produced; it is about distribution – how people get a share in what is produced. Everything from trade policies to government projects to commercial regulations will in the future be evaluated by distribution. Politics will change, free-market beliefs will change, social structures will change. We are still at the start of this shift, but it will be deep and will unfold indefinitely in the future."

Maybe. Few firms may well remain dominant in many industries exercising a high degree of influence and control and thus 'rationing' access – with perhaps the additional use of decentralized structures for some forms of 'last mile' distribution. If it is local exchange being examined, it is very different if it's on the basis of a formal, bureaucratic, probably cashless system where it is hard to accommodate the real peer-to-peer economy.

As an example, the buying and selling of second hand goods is impossible with the welfare card currently being trialled in Australia, and no purchases of alcohol or cigarettes are 'sanctioned' even at authorized retailers[5]. Social credit systems already in place in parts of China also speak of conditional access to a whole range of goods and services – such as train tickets, or even shopping malls[6]. It might be that, in future, the question of distribution is very much placed ahead of production but both could be highly structured and exclusive, far from entrepreneurial and not in the spirit of freedom and security as proposed by some basic dividend advocates – including ourselves. This would be grudging welfare instead. In this system there would be little but informal exchange on a devolved level – 'System D', or resourcefulness, as the French describe it[7].

This sort of distributed future implies that scarcity is still a system outcome, it's a design or default of 'how the world works', despite the changes proposed.

But a universal basic dividend designed in the spirit of freedom and security looks somewhat different: people without a full-time job are valued citizens, of equal status to anyone, say, with a full time job, and able to access publicly supported infrastructure without any hindrance or conditions and which freedoms then give that possibility to flourish. And food production, processing and exchange? That needs to flourish alongside the basic rules around distribution and access. Perhaps for the first time, there is also the question of the role of cash. Cash is anonymous. Cash is provided by the state as a medium of exchange and as vote of confidence in, as well as an obligation to, the individual in the structure of a basic dividend. A basic dividend as both unconditional as to who gets it and unconditional on how they spend it. Here citizen... make your choices! This is all about the state as enabler rather than operator of the panopticon, aided by so-called 'surveillance capitalism'[8]. The state as enabler is fundamental to the aspiration for something good to come out of a well designed economy which is 'regenerative, accessible and abundant'. In the end, this is not just about resources and a circular economy, it's about people and democracy. Even if the macroeconomic rules of the game as we have already described are in place – such as a debt jubilee, a basic dividend and tax-shifting to moderate the influence of the rentier – they can all be perverted by something as simple as setting a too low basic dividend. This then forces individuals into low paid additional employment and if a cashless but conditional service is used the purchases of specified goods and services are proscribed. Indeed why not apply both as a means of looking progressive while in reality punishing the recipients?

This is the crux of dealing with systems; unintended consequences can spin off and undermine the good intentions of the system designers or systems can be gamed. That's why it is vital to get the system conditions right, including certain core principles like seeking freedom and autonomy – not control and dependency. And not locking in any of the system conditions and principles too soon really matters.

In a remarkable experiment everyone can do at home, if they want, it's possible to show how systems can be entrained or captured by altering the way feedback is managed. The example can be used positively or negatively – as in the above scenario around cash and social credit. The individual element is subtly, indirectly, entrained.

In this 90 second video[9] five mechanical metronomes on a foam/fibre board are set running, each working away out of sync with every other. But move the board onto two empty drinks cans and in under a minute the metronomes are synchronised. Systems coupled like this change and no individual decision is needed. The emergent property of synchronisation results from feedback entraining the system.

Mark Blyth, the economist, suggests that, by analogy to the drinks cans under the metronomes board, this is the role of macroeconomics – to create an entraining framework of synchronised relationships for the economy and that role is crucial[10]. As a shared

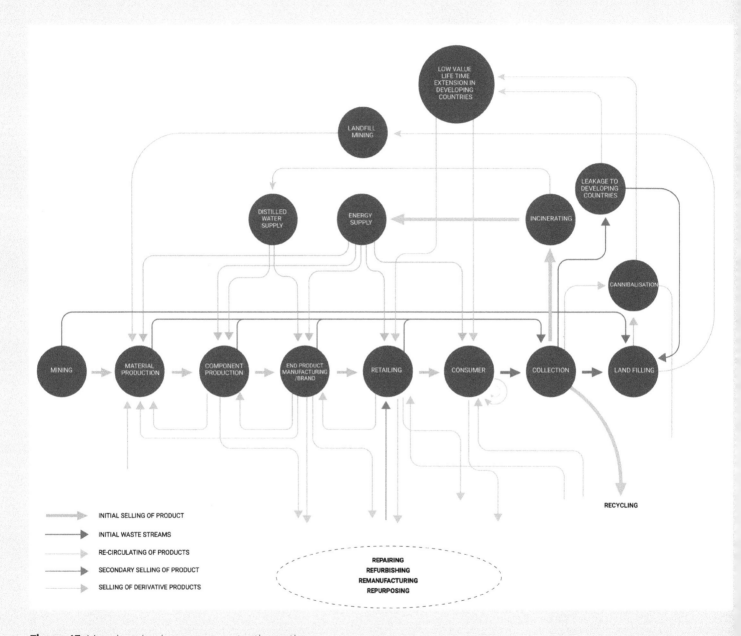

Figure 43: Mapping circular economy retention options

Adapted from: Denise Reike[11]

Illustration: Graham Pritchard

narrative about the basic relationships and assumptions, macro-economics can be incredibly powerful. *But, as we have discussed above, none of this is in the absence of politics, it is a great error to see a circular economy as a neutral technological exercise.*

It's pertinent when it comes to the idea of a circular economy because a circular economy, currently, is often cited as an approach to 'how we produce'. This kind of circular economy comes with some pretty strong assumptions about the context for 'slowing the flow' and 'closing the loop' in the production system: production is centralised; there is a high concentration of ownership in the industry and it's 'at scale'; it's dominated by large scale production at a relatively few centres; and production is done efficiently, including resource efficiency of course. Currently, the circular economy is usually seen as more about the formal economy rather than the informal. In a way, the materials flow diagram in figure 43 is pretty much built on this overarching set of assumptions, even if it is not visible (the authors do talk about this bias)[11]. The clues are everywhere in the language of 'businesses and consumers' and the suggestion of large flows – 'land fill', 'recycling' and incineration.

No wonder city governments and other urban development stakeholders might look at the version of a circular economy illustrated in figure 43 and wonder two things: what does this mean apart from a cleaner city and some more jobs (welcome as it is); and, at first sight, this diagram gives the impression that circular economy is not about economic development or community building per se so much *as improving the plumbing of the material flows.*

But if production, distribution and access gets easier due to technological innovation then the economy can become (as we hinted above) more decentralised. Then, perhaps, it will enable the positive feedback loops of the circular materials economy to be more effective as tighter, shorter loops are possible. The economy might also then go some way along the path to being monetarily as well as physically distributive – the value created circulates more locally and directly between producer and consumer/user for many categories of goods and service. The roles people play might then be more fluid: 'prosumers', producers not just consumers for example[12]; and the unpaid or informal economy fits right in the mix as something positive rather than something to be colonised by the use of new technologies or marginalized by a drive towards a cashless system. In this situation, the surplus, in a competitive entrepreneurial sense is not great – the surplus needs to be distributed to many players and many users and consumers. A surplus is not there to be extracted but will be reinjected into the local economy, through *exchange*: at least that is what being distributive implies. Adam Smith would be pleased (a free market, for him, was one free from the landlord or middle man leveraging and profiting from scarcity). As would circular economy pioneer Gunter Pauli[13] for whom changing business models and an entre-preneurial approach have always been key. He has extolled and practiced the virtues of building a new economy from the base for over 20 years:

> *"Business models that respond to people's basic needs with what is locally available could improve livelihoods. However, the money earned cannot be drained out of the community, as is the case now. Rather, the hard-earned funds should continue to circulate within the communities. If people have earned one hundred dollars, then this cash is used to alleviate their most urgent needs. The money must be spent locally and the most very basic needs should be sourced locally as well; this creates a catalytic effect in the local growth cycle. As more money circulates faster, the locally produced portfolio of products and services diversify further so that added money moves faster and more is kept in the local community as capital. The double-digit growth model [will] :*

> • respond to basic needs
> • with local products and services
> • circulate the cash in the local economy"[13]

Here, Gunter Pauli overlaps with the world of Paul Mason and Jeremy Rifkind – and perhaps Brian Arthur – where they argue that falling marginal costs of everything can potentially build a diverse and productive economy underneath the existing one, much like the rich layers of soil and humus in a forest. The richness doesn't come from a materials economy *per se* but from a shifting kind of economic development which takes advantage of the circulation of materials, the regeneration of natural and social capital, the circulation of value, the circulation of money city-wide, the development of skills and having access to resources, tools and infrastructure which are capital building. Yes, materials matter very much and are a potential source of value if 'waste can become food'. Here is what this kind of economic development can feed upon. The practice now is fragmentary and diffuse but, if Brian Arthur is right, the changes beginning to take place in the economy will be deep and "will unfold indefinitely..." He is talking about possible entrainment, the way that technology has changed and will change system conditions for a new economy. It sounds like magic, but as demonstrated in the metronomes example, the system design is about the positioning of the metronomes and the choice of coupling – the table or the coke cans. Just leaving the metronomes on a big table is a connected but not a 'coupled' system as it's not able to transmit the vibrations – the feedback which entrains the system. Some of this harks back to taking insights from living systems. Gunter Pauli again: "nature responds to basic needs and then evolves from sufficiency to abundance. The present economic model relies on scarcity as a basis for production and consumption."

Figure 44: Setting up a maker lab tools workshop

Photo credit: POC21

This is where cities and cities governance comes back into focus. If cities wish to see Brian Arthur's unfoldment happen swiftly, and in a positive way or with as little friction as possible, then it has to be able and willing to create that loosely coupled, decentralised and distributive infrastructure, and ... to wait. Waiting means observing how providing this infrastructure affects the coupling, the feedback and then adjusting accordingly. It does not mean *engineering* solutions for people. It means to take on wise governance which, as the author of the Tao De Ching wrote is "like cooking a small fish" (it needs attention and sensitive adjustment to prevent the food being ruined). The small shards of this changing urban economy are visible (they are not even coherent enough yet to be called 'green shoots') in the appearance of maker labs, platform cooperatives, community kitchens, 'pay-what-its-worth' cafes, food surplus Company Shops, alternative complementary currencies, peri-urban market gardens, distributed local energy nets and LiFi[14].

The trick is that in this distributive urban economy being "regenerative, accessible and abundant" – a favourite shorthand created by Lucy Hardy at the Ellen MacArthur Foundation – means amplifying the potential of people, entrepreneurs, the social entrepreneurs, the non-profits, cooperatives and commons organisations by providing places, tools, materials and connections as well as harnessing the education and skills potentials of the city population.

The fastest growing group in society belongs to the 'precariat' – as Guy Standing describes them[15] – not the fully employed middle class 'salariat', which is shrinking in developed nations. A by-product of the existing system is growing inequality, this expanding precariat, the gig economy and the working poor, which in bald terms mean a fall in spending power. An approach which recognizes this situation has a big advantage over one which cleaves to an outdated reality. A rump of the salariat fearful of their loss of status would probably not support an inclusive approach at all and we can see narrow boundaries and more naked self interest in the politics of the day than for a couple of decades. This has to be overcome in order to keep the economy vibrant – to create, at its crudest, the customers that business needs, to truly value creativity and entrepreneurial effort, and to reinvigorate the real economy.

A new infrastructure itself is necessary but not systemically sufficient. The more radical difference might be the channeling of a universal basic dividend – derived from national decisions – with a local, city, currency as one tranche of it. Out of this rich soil grows a distributive-by-design economy. Whether it is a basic dividend or some variation like a job guarantee or universal basic services is currently an active and fierce debate and reflects differing notions of what is possible, or deserved, or the political background of the proposer. The left tend to look at paternal offerings – basic services or job guarantees for example. But the key question to ask is: "in systems terms, what fits best with the deep changes towards a distribution-led system that have been observed by Brian Arthur and others?"

Deciding the basic macroeconomic narrative underlying a prosperous urban economy seems to be an important task if we are to create the synchronous and positive development so many seek. Or to avoid the pitchforks and social upheaval, if you are more pessimistic. In terms of ideas about foundation relationships, it does not get much more fundamental than "where does wealth come from?" Is this an economy based on the idea that wealth comes from use not ownership and from the use of the commons rather than their enclosure by private individuals or organisations? And is this an economy where demand creates its own supply not the other way around? It's a subject with a long history of debate for sure but has surfaced in the 'post-industrial' era afresh. Michel Bauwens points out that the benefits of the commons are not just around resources. Mai Sutton writes in *Shareable*[16]:

"Bauwens says that with any commons project, urban or otherwise, there are two major potential benefits of having people share and govern over a common resource. The first is that it can reduce the environmental and material footprint of that community. With any physical commons, people can mutually share and provision its use. Instead of having many people buy or own their own car or tools for example, they can share it, leading to less of those goods having to be produced or transported in the first place. The second potential of the commons is that they can help build a true democracy, or what Bauwens calls a 'school for democracy'. When people have to govern something together, they need to make decisions collectively and work together. The commons is where people can practice and exercise their civic muscles by talking and meeting with other members of their community face-to-face."

Figure 45 (opposite page):

Circular economy – for transition or transformation?

Adapted from: Kate Raworth[19]

Illustration: Graham Pritchard

We come back to the core. Does it matter which kind of circular economy you have in mind? It seems so. It might depend on whether cities are seeking transition or transformation. In the former situation, the idea is to find an economic and business case for treating resources (materials and energy) differently while spinning off environmental and social benefits – the social element being achieved largely through additional spending in the economy brought by resource efficiency and then new jobs. It's the message within books like *Good Disruption*[17] and reports like *Growth Within*[18] (from the Ellen MacArthur Foundation). It is about economic growth opportunities compared to a wasteful business as usual. In the latter situation, the idea of transformation, the assumption is that the Economy (big E) pretty much doesn't work for most people right now and going circular is about contributing to something more profound: a way of building an economy by changing the system conditions. But how the 'system' is conceived is important since this encompasses the framework for thinking underlying the conception. This goes deep.

In her widely read book *Doughnut Economics*[19], Kate Raworth's exploration of economic ideas and their roots seems to confirm this general sense. In the left hand column of figure 45 is her distillation of mainstream economic 'habits of thought' which share something of the basic worldview or metaphor of 'world as machine' or 'world as mechanism'. In the 20th century economics column of figure 45 the economic ideas are around markets and its discipline. These ideas also echo George Lakoff's idea of seeing 'nation as family'[20]. Here that's demonstrated in its 'strict parent' and conservative orientation in that if individuals learn to fit the ideal the economy sets us, then the economy will reward those who contribute, in relation to the effort made. It is just. It is also orientated around production efficiency, prompted by competition, as this is the means to meet the end – economic growth – by which all are rewarded.

	FROM 20TH CENTURY ECONOMICS Circular economy as a transition; fixes materials/resources, harnesses digital feedback?	**TO 21ST CENTURY ECONOMICS** Circular economy as one part of a transformation: using dynamic systems insights with materials/resources as Step 1?
7 WAYS TO THINK		
1 CHANGE THE GOAL	GDP	THE DOUGHNUT
2 SEE THE BIG PICTURE	SELF-CONTAINED MARKET	EMBEDDED ECONOMY
3 NURTURE HUMAN NATURE	RATIONAL ECONOMIC MAN	SOCIAL ADAPTABLE HUMANS
4 GET SAVVY WITH SYSTEMS	MECHANICAL EQUILIBRIUM	DYNAMIC COMPLEXITY
5 DESIGN TO DISTRIBUTE	GROWTH WILL EVEN IT UP AGAIN	DISTRIBUTIVE BY DESIGN
6 CREATE TO REGENERATE	GROWTH WILL CLEAN IT UP AGAIN	REGENERATE BY DESIGN
7 BE AGNOSTIC ABOUT GROWTH	GROWTH ADDICTED	GROWTH AGNOSTIC

In the right hand column of this illustration are shifts based on a more expansive and transformative context – less the discipline and more what Lakoff calls the nurturing family notion of the nation so to speak – expressed through the idea of not just efficiency but overall harmony in the nation as family, its *effectiveness*. This is a system-wide functioning derived from the notion that since the system iterates with indeterminacy built in – it has many actors who have agency ('all the family matters') – then even if it's a closed system (to materials anyway, at the boundary) it will reveal connection, be open and be distributive throughout. Unsurprisingly, this mode of thought is not best described as pipework/plumbing or machine-like; that's to invoke the 'closed loop' as control. Too deterministic. It has to be based on a different metaphor, one which captures effective, dynamic, flexible, inclusive. We have suggested that it's a living systems orientation and the metaphors are usually around effective living systems: ecosystems, gardens, forests, sometimes organisms (like the human body), bloodstreams. In this mode, ideas which are aimed at effective circulation at all scales pop up frequently (since large and small are fundamentally interdependent). The intuitive element is part of the argument and possibly the wider attraction of the phrase 'circular economy' because it speaks of maintaining systems intact long term – the capital from which flows are derived, as well as the flow itself. Even Adam Smith who spoke about the way wealth was created talked of 'the great circulation'. There is satisfaction in the concept of closing the loop coupled with regeneration and renewal (rather than control).

In *Doughnut Economics* Kate Raworth calls this overall shift to a devolved participatory approach 'distributive by design'. She puts this side by side with 'regenerative by design' as two key elements of a 21st century approach. In a recent development, she is also increasingly contrasting open and closed loops in TV appearances by drawing on the 'pipework' versus 'network' conceptions.

The impact of coherent narrative around change is startling, once the initial worldview is shifted to one that's reflective on what science is telling us about open loop, networked connectivity being the dominant mode. It's a reminder that science matters and that these things should be informed, evidence-based approaches rather than belief or faith-based. Then different kinds of ideas and solutions present themselves. This is particularly relevant to how cities and their infrastructure are envisaged in an enabled systems perspective. This shift in worldview encourages action and participation since a regenerative, open source and inclusive circular economy sounds like one which is enabling rather than one to where only the fittest will be rewarded (the people who fit the discipline of the existing but troubled economy).

If the likes of Yuval Harari[21] are right, it is the shared stories, the myths which enable broader change. Currently, the existing mainstream narrative around the circular economy is firmly fixed within an efficiency and growth proposal. It is strongly orientated towards a transition, to fix up what is amiss with the materials/resources. In diagrammatic form it might look like the left hand column in figure 45: compare that with the right hand column which illustrates the normal circular economy narrative extended into a circular economy for transformation narrative.

A key element of all this is being able to share and share in the outcome of the story being presented, and to do it in a way that connects emotionally. Eric Beinhocker, the internationally renowned complexity economist, and Nick Hanauer, the self-styled business plutocrat, have taken the shift in metaphor seriously[22]. They imagine the economy transformed, as the economy is fitted to nature and not the other way around. They seek to remake capitalism for our times. They are the systems thinkers in a more profound sense, accepting participation and influence rather than control and capture:

"This recent Copernican-like shift in perspective provides a powerful new framework for understanding how and why capitalism works, what wealth truly is, and where growth comes from. This 21st century way to understand economics allows us to understand capitalism as an evolutionary problem-solving system. It allows us to see that the solutions capitalism produces are what create real prosperity in people's lives, and the rate at which we create solutions is true economic growth. This perspective also allows us to see that good moral choices will be the ones that create true prosperity. This new perspective also makes obvious why both the laissez-faire policies of the far right and the statism of the far left fail. Policies that provide opportunities for all citizens to fulfill their potential, and investments that enable them to expand their potential, are the surest ways to animate prosperity and growth. Recognizing the ecosystem-like nature of economies highlights the essential feedback loop between businesses and customers. Policy must aim to create customers as well as entrepreneurs, and to create as many of these feedback loops as possible."[22]

So is it circular economy for transition or circular economy for transformation in our cities? Really? Does it matter? Probably if the winners are those who tell the most persuasive story then, paradoxically, the circular economy is a winner either way. There is a 'but'....

If the circular economy is a technical fix then it buys time and is a practical help, and of business interest, but a circular economy's longer term fate depends on whether it is a harbinger of wider change. In this sense, a circular economy cannot lose *provided*

the sense of progression is maintained through being quite explicit that the core of circularity is a thoroughgoing systems perspective, and one which is consistent with the insights from living systems, not mechanical systems. This biological/ecological perspective is one which must extend to the very habits of thought of economists (see figure 45). A living systems orientation is both the grounding of the existing and the source of ambition for the possible. So different circular economy narratives can be more than variations on a theme because they derive from different frameworks for thinking.

Any definitive conclusion here would be a falsity – it's a dynamic feedback-rich interplay of systems after all. But a snapshot of the circular cities discussion would include recognising the way the economic system is shifting towards this issue of 'distributive by design' – alongside the traditional circular economy shorthand of 'regenerative by design'. This is an inevitable shift according to Brian Arthur and others – he argues, remember, that "everything… will, in the future, be evaluated by distribution". The evidence is substantial.

Equally, it is important to recognise that setting the underlying macroeconomic narrative and system conditions can entrain and shape the outcomes within that profound shift and this is, and always has been, a role for cities themselves. But nowadays, we argue, city governance should be about an 'enabler' approach – creating that loosely coupled and distributed infrastructure, then observing feedback and coupling, then adjusting as required. In this emerging era, it looks more like the priority for city governance is to enable the growing precariat to remake the economy from the ground up. The need is to create foundations, rather than assuming that the middle class and business growing together will be able to support taxation for a state or city-level 'safety net' for the few who cannot match, or have fallen short in, the existing rules of the game.

Opposite page: perhaps the symbol of regeneration will be a systems reminder

There is a world of difference in talking 'foundations' rather than a 'safety net'. It is, as always, a changing mindset which can liberate us to see different options, and different uses for the notion of a circular economy, and the roots of the thinking which is, broadly speaking, 'circularity' – a feedback-rich system perspective. And a different mindset is more importantly positive when it comes to maintaining and perhaps refurbishing democracy for a contemporary age. The Romans, in one of the original city states, stamped SPQR everywhere (Senātus Populus que Rōmānus...By the order of the Senate and People of Rome).

Chapter references and notes

1. Wang, W., Themelis, N.J., and Sun, K. (2019). Current influence of China's ban on plastic waste imports. *Waste Dispos. Sustain. Energy*, 1, pp. 67–78 https://doi.org/10.1007/s42768-019-00005-z

2. Baran, P. (1964). On distributed communications. Memorandum, August 1964. The Rand Corporation

https://www.rand.org/content/dam/rand/pubs/research_memoranda/2006/RM3420.pdf

3. Alexander, C. (1965). A City is Not a Tree. *Architectural Forum*, 122, No 1, April 1965, pp. 58-62 (Part I). Also volume 122, No 2, May 1965, pp. 58-62 (Part II)

https://www.patternlanguage.com/archive/cityisnotatree.html

4. Arthur, W. B. *Where is technology taking the economy?* (2017)

https://www.mckinsey.com/business-functions/mckinsey-analytics/our-insights/where-is-technology-taking-the-economy

5. Henriques-Gomes, L. (2020). Cashless welfare card: how does it work and what changes is the government proposing? *The Guardian*

https://www.theguardian.com/australia-news/2020/feb/06/cashless-welfare-card-how-does-it-work-and-what-changes-is-the-government-proposing

6. Botsman, R. (2017). Big Data meets Big Brother as China moves to rate its citizens. *Wired magazine*

https://www.wired.co.uk/article/chinese-government-social-credit-score-privacy-invasion

7. 'System D', or resourcefulness, as the French describe it: a loose entrepreneurial system built around the edges of what is legal but pervasive for all that will work with cash circulating in a sophisticated black market.

8. McMullan, T. (2015). What does the panopticon mean in the age of digital surveillance? *The Guardian*

https://www.theguardian.com/technology/2015/jul/23panopticon-digital-surveillance-jeremy-bentham

9. 90 second video of mechanical metronomes on a foam/fibre board

https://www.youtube.com/watch?v=Aaxw4zbULMs

10. Mark Blyth on metronomes at around 14.35 to 17.50 on the video https://www.youtube.com/watch?v=iq3s-lfxlFo Talk entitled: *Why Do People Continue To Believe Stupid Economic Ideas?* (2017)

11. Reike, D., Vermeulen, W. and Witjes, S. (2018). The circular economy: New or Refurbished as CE 3.0? Exploring Controversies in the Conceptualization of the Circular Economy through a Focus on History and Resource Value Retention Options. *Resources, Conservation and Recycling*, 135

http://programme.exordo.com/isdrs2017/delegates/presentation/320/

12. Prosumers. From Alvin Toffler's book *The Third Wave* (1980) though the meaning has shifted over time. In this item it means able to produce as well as being an involved consumer. For discussion see https://medium.com/@aditya.vikram/the-rise-of-prosumers-and-what-it-means-for-consumer-companies-26d408325934

13. Pauli, G. *Blue Growth: Reflections on How to Get Out of The Poverty and Jobless Trap through a Bottom-Up Scenario*. (2015) http://www.gunterpauli.com/blog/blue-growth

14, Li-Fi (short for light fidelity) is wireless communication technology which utilizes light to transmit data and position between devices.

15. Guy Standing on universal basic income. Four minute interview clip (2017) https://www.youtube.com/watch?v=EkHV6bkycXI

16. Sutton, M. *Ghent's quick rise as a sustainable commons-based sharing city*. (2017) https://www.shareable.net/blog/ghents-quick-rise-as-a-sustainable-commons-based-sharing-city

17. Stuchtey, M., Zumwinkel, K. and Enkvist, P. *A Good Disruption: Redefining Growth in the Twenty-First Century*. Bloomsbury. (2016)

18. Ellen Macarthur Foundation. *Growth Within: a circular economy vision for a competitive Europe*. (2015)

19. Raworth, K. *Doughnut Economics: Seven Ways to Think Like a 21st-Century Economist* . RH Business Books. (2017)

The 'Doughnut', or 'Doughnut economics', is a visual framework for sustainable development – shaped like a doughnut – combining the concept of planetary boundaries with the complementary concept of social boundaries.

Also see this BBC video about doughnut economics in the city of Amsterdam:

https://www.bbc.com/reel/video/p08hppxt/how-the-dutch-are-reshaping-their-post-pandemic-utopia

20. Patricia McBroom of University of California at Berkeley introduces George Lakoff's metaphor of a 'nation as family'.

https://www.berkeley.edu/news/berkeleyan/1996/0828/politic.html

21. Harari, Y. *Sapiens: A Brief History of Humankind*. Harper Collins. (2015)

22. Hanauer, N. and Beinhocker, E. (2014). Capitalism redefined. *Democracy*, Winter No. 31 https://democracyjournal.org/magazine/31/capitalism-redefined/

23. *Disintermediation* means the removal of intermediaries in economics from a supply chain, or 'cutting out the middlemen' in connection with a transaction or a series of transactions

24. Elliott, L. (2020). The British government is about to sleepwalk into an unemployment crisis. *The Guardian*

https://www.theguardian.com/commentisfree/2020/jun/25/government-britain-unemployment-crisis-rishi-sunak-furlough-jobs

CHAPTER 6

FOOD SYSTEMS IN CITIES

"Cities ... need all kinds of diversity, intricately mingled in mutual support. They need this so city life can work decently and constructively, and so the people of cities can sustain ... their society and civilization. ... I think that the science of city planning ... must become the science and art of catalysing and nourishing diverse, close-grained working
relationships that support each other economically and socially".
Jane Jacobs, *Cities and the Wealth of Nations*[28]

It's interesting if you look at Thomas More's *Utopia,* written in the 16th century, as a sort of critique of London at the time – it was already growing big as a city because it was on a navigable river. Thomas More invents this imaginary world called Utopia where people live in a series of semi-independent city states – limited in size to about 30,000 – arranged in a network, so that every city was about a day's walk from every other one. In More's Utopia everyone loved food. They had gardening competitions and everybody farmed – men, women and children farmed. It was the only activity that everybody in Utopia got involved with![1].

An early 20th century example of an urban and peri-urban food utopia features in the architect Ebenezer Howard's *Garden City*. It looks a bit like Thomas More's utopia – but with railways (figure 47). He said we need to stop building these big metropolitan areas and, instead, develop a series of semi-independent city states, limited in size. He also comes up with an ideal city size of 32,000, with one capital of 58,000 citizens. And all of these cities would have dedicated farmland around them, held in trust for the cities so when land prices rose the city would actually benefit. Caroline Steel, author of *Hungry City*[1] comments on this radical model: "[Ebenezer Howard's utopia] couldn't be farther apart from what we think of as 'garden cities', which is kind of pretty suburbia with nice cottagey looking houses and of course the irony is that you know, cities, garden cities like Letchworth did get built but not according to Howard's modelling. In fact, he stormed out in protest off the project because the bit they didn't do was the really important bit which was having the dedicated agricultural land actually considered part of the city." It seems a serious bout of corporate capture of the 'garden city' idea took place in those town planning meetings in the 1930s!

Figure 46 (opposite page): Thomas More's Utopia Source: British Library

Moving to the 21st-century ....as we try to develop a picture of distributed regenerative food systems in and around cities we need to grapple with a number of elements. Here are just a few: enabler government setting the macroeconomic enabling conditions; regenerative farms and market gardens using biomimetic design principles such as 'waste=food' and 'celebrate diversity'; the regeneration of soil, as the critical natural capital of our food systems; distributed food enterprises working together, cooperating as well as competing within local and regional food networks.

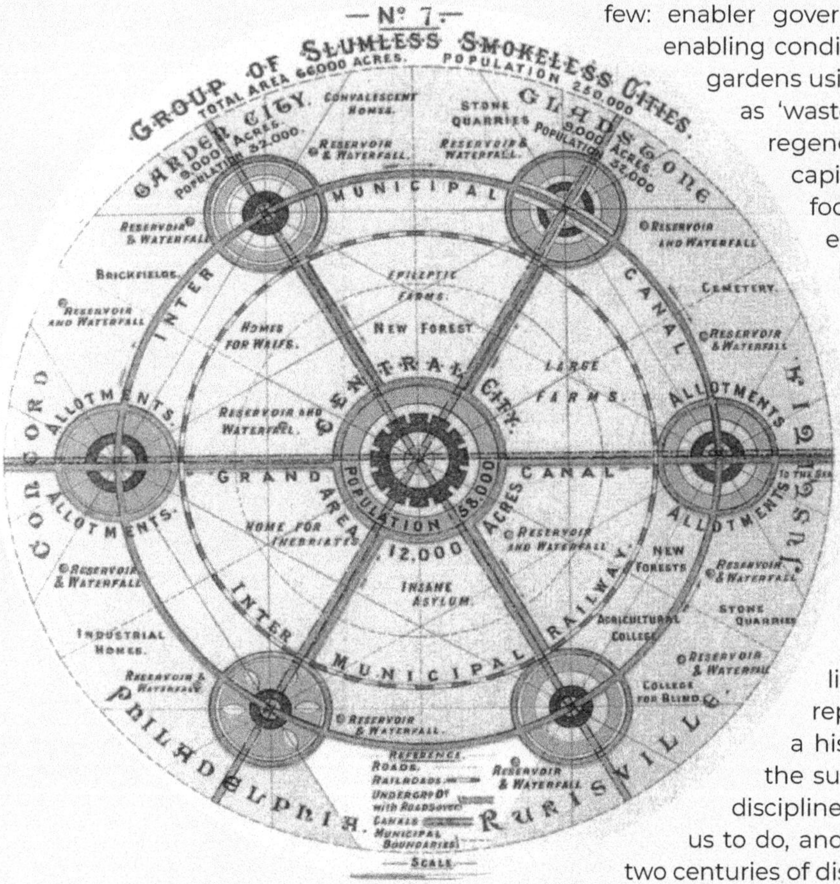

How best to visualise these future food systems in cities? For now, let's stay with utopias as a tool for envisioning. It can be a helpful approach. As Caroline Steel says, utopias themselves may not be achievable but they can be used to inspire a vision of a better society. She sees utopia as "a philosophical tool, a parallel universe whose chief purpose is to ask what an ideal society might look like". Steel observes that "utopianism represents the nearest thing we have to a history of cross-disciplinary thought on the subject of human dwelling. Thinking in disciplines is what the Enlightenment taught us to do, and that's very useful, up to a point. But two centuries of disciplined thought have given us architecture, planning, economics, sociology, politics, geography, ecology etc. each capable of operating in a virtual vacuum. What they have not given us is a way of thinking about dwelling holistically. Utopianism is at least an attempt to do that."[1].

Figure 47: Ebenezer Howard's 'Garden City' 1930

Source: Ebenezer Howard

So let's try a small thought experiment.... it's 2030 and Europe now boasts a dense network of local and regional regenerative food innovation hubs. One such regional hub is in the county of Yorkshire in Northern England. Here a food and housing revolution is underway in the cities and market towns which are connected by the region's purpose-built food digital network. This open source online platform[2], which developed in under a decade, is at the heart of the region's food innovation activities: individual city and town governments use the platform to manage and administer their own supplementary version of a universal basic dividend – they call this a 'beetroot bond'[3] with £40 per month available to every citizen to purchase local food. In addition, there is a large food innovation funding pot, established using income generated from a new land value tax; residents in different communities use this software to connect directly with nearby food producers and to vote on budget allocations for their community food projects; and universities in the region are in online dialogue with small, medium and large-sized food enterprises about their collaborative food research projects.

Yorkshire's universal 'beetroot bond' and business innovation fund have released a wave of enterprising and community-led food projects. This new food economy has co-evolved around a regional housing revolution after architects and town planners worked with communities to envision and design housing using so-called 'participatory futures techniques'[4]. In 2030 there is now housing choice and depending on taste, you can live in a well-designed terrace, a suburb, a tower, a bungalow, mansion block, concrete council estate, squat or hostel. Your home can be old or new, designed perhaps by one of the region's young architects[5]. Nationally, house prices have stopped rising, with the result that they have gradually become more affordable as incomes go up. There are more homes to rent at affordable prices. New housing has been planned around shared open gardens, allotments and green space commons so as to boost leisure and recreation opportunities as well as household-level food growing initiatives. Schools and shops are within walking distance, and there is little need for cars, especially as integrated transport options are available.

Designed in parallel to this housing revolution, in 2030 a wealth of diverse food enterprises have grown up to supply healthy, affordable food[6] for the residents of Yorkshire's towns and cities.

Around the 'intensified suburbs'[5] of York and Leeds a chain of two hectare regenerative market gardens use high-technology sowing, planting and harvesting techniques to produce huge quantities of pesticide-free salad greens, tomatoes and cucumbers – growing crops for most of the year, unheated polytunnels on these market gardens yield over 100 tonnes of salad greens per hectare per year[7] (figure 48). These 'intensified suburbs' in the outer city boroughs have good public transport and the old two-storey housing has been complemented with the construction of new four to five-storey buildings. These high-density populations means more business for local shops and restaurants – key outlets for the new peri-urban market gardens.

Across the region there has been huge growth in community land trusts, food and farming cooperatives and co-housing projects – at the heart of all these initiatives is the idea that projects are run on behalf of the community where profits are recirculated within the communities – for community benefit. In the cities of Sheffield and Bradford there are now hundreds of 20-house clusters built as co-housing developments made of locally sourced wheat straw bales and timber and designed to capture and store the heat of the sun. Residents in these clusters share green spaces such as allotments, ponds, woodlands and orchards as well as 'a common house' for communal meals, laundry, films and other community-based activities. These housing clusters feature the 'allotment +' model, where fruit and vegetables are grown as usual for individual household use but at the same time excess allotment produce and apples from community orchards are harvested, prepared, cooked and preserved as a basis for developing skills and enterprise alongside a new community kitchen and temporary food store (not a food bank). Larger regenerative 3-D apple orchards have been established on under-used urban common land and these feature apple tree varieties that suit the local soil and climatic conditions: Yorkshire Beauty; Yorkshire Aromatic; Dog's Snout; Flower of the Town; Grandpa Buxton; Fillingham Pippin – in the year 2030, the apple harvest is bountiful.

Figure 48: Organically grown salad greens from unheated polytunnels

Credit: Growing with Grace

Apple harvest

Meanwhile, a Yorkshire Dales farmers cooperative in 2030 is advising the Leeds city government on how to develop holistic management grazing techniques to graze sheep on the city's Roundhay Park. The council has leased, at low cost, 200 hectares of the parkland for a start-up sheep farm – Swaledale farmers and Leeds University business lecturers are working with the start-up farmer and her shepherds to hone holistic management, sheep-dog training, business model and meat/wool marketing skills.

In Bradford's huge 19th century Victorian cotton mills, architects have designed a high-density mix of affordable flats, open cafes and open source workshops where people pool machine tools and other production machinery in shared spaces. 'Hydroponic farms' have been established within the cotton mills – covering an area of 10 football pitches – the indoor lighting for the hydroponic system is powered by renewable energy and the solar panels on the roofs feature the highly efficient new perovskite crystals[8]. Nutrients for the lettuce, tomatoes, cucumbers and other salad crops grown hydroponically comes from locally sourced and processed soldier fly compost (avoiding the need for fossil fuel-based fertilisers used in first-generation hydroponic farms).

Figure 49 (above): Perovskite crystal
Photo credit: vevoevale

Figure 50 (below): Food waste-soldier fly composting cycle

Adapted from: Agriprotein[9]

Illustration: Graham Pritchard

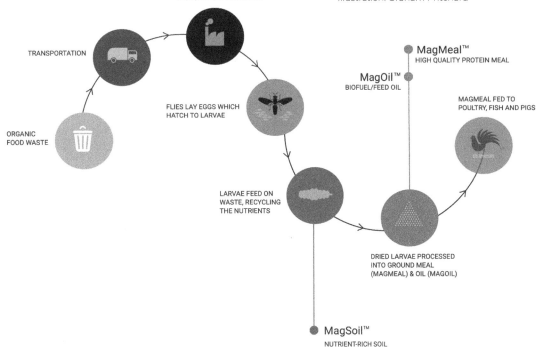

FACTORY FOR PROCESSING

TRANSPORTATION

FLIES LAY EGGS WHICH
HATCH TO LARVAE

ORGANIC
FOOD WASTE

LARVAE FEED ON
WASTE, RECYCLING
THE NUTRIENTS

DRIED LARVAE PROCESSED
INTO GROUND MEAL
(MAGMEAL) & OIL (MAGOIL)

MagMeal™
HIGH QUALITY PROTEIN MEAL

MagOil™
BIOFUEL/FEED OIL

MAGMEAL FED TO
POULTRY, FISH AND PIGS

MagSoil™
NUTRIENT-RICH SOIL

Figure 51: Low-impact living affordable community (LILAC), Leeds, England. This co-housing development of 20 homes – with a 'common house' – features straw bale and timber houses clustered around community allotments, a pond and play area[11]

Photo credit: Andy Lord

There are huge food material flows through the region so in South Yorkshire Sheffield and Doncaster are piloting a distributed network of food composting centres – billions of soldier flies are farmed at these centres, the fly larvae feeding on the household and restaurant kitchen 'waste' that is collected from the region. Fly larvae are then harvested and used as feed for chickens, fish and pigs. A by-product called 'Magsoil' is an excellent soil conditioner/fertiliser[9,10] and returns biological nutrients back to the peri-urban farmland around Sheffield.

Perhaps the Yorkshire 2030 housing revolution sketched here is just too utopian? Not according to the respected architect and journalist Rowan Moore. In his report *A blueprint for British housing 2028*[5] he describes how radical housing designs, tools and ideas are already here: "...most are already being put success-fully into practice. To be sure, their application tends to be small-scale and piecemeal. What is lacking is a concerted political will to turn valiant and thoughtful initiatives into a programme that could transform millions of lives." For Rowan Moore, a prerequisite to achieve nationwide application of radical housing programmes is to shift away from the current thinking that housebuilding should always be led by big business – instead, a diverse mix of additional housing providers is required: community groups; local government; housing associations and small-scale builders.

And what about this 2030 utopia for an urban and peri-urban food and farming revolution in Yorkshire…. far-fetched? Perhaps not. New food production systems, tools and ideas are here now – they are being applied successfully around the world but have not yet scaled out. As we discussed in chapter 2, that's primarily because the macroeconomic enabling conditions (such as universal basic dividend and radical tax shifts) and the devolved and distributed food economy infrastructure (e.g. community kitchens, temporary food stores) are so slow to catch up. Yet it's not an exaggeration to say that a thousand flowers are blooming right now when it comes to regenerative food and farming enterprises, systems and technologies. To give just a flavour...

In Québec, Canada on the rich alluvial soils of the River Hudson there is a one hectare organic market garden called the *Jardins de la Grelinette*. Inspired by the mass of market gardens that surrounded 19th-century Paris (box 5), throughout spring, summer, autumn and the harsh Quebec winters Jean-Martin Fortier supplies Montreal's restaurants and 200 families with abundant supplies of salad greens, tomatoes, cucumbers, baby turnips and more. Sowing, planting, weeding, harvesting and washing all these crops for market is hard work but through careful soil regeneration techniques and the introduction of state-of-the-art labour saving tools, his salad greens reach impressive yields. This one hectare market garden generates an annual turnover of 130,000 Canadian dollars. To match these figures, conventional market gardening would require an area five times as big. His regenerative model enables him to generate a net profit margin of 46%. Jean-Martin explains: "I don't use the quality of my system to harvest more.

BOX 2

MARKET GARDENS, PARIS 1850-1900

Influential American market gardener, Elliot Coleman, has been inspired by the market gardens of historic Paris:

La culture maraichere (market gardening) in Paris from the 1850s was the impressive result of years of improvement in both protected and outdoor vegetable production. Those early beginnings (from 1670s) reach their impressive climax in the hands of the Parisian maraichers (market gardeners) between 1850 and 1900. The average size market garden at the time was between one and two acres in size. The cultivated land of the Parisian.growers covered up to 6% of all the land within the city limits of Paris. In order to maximise production per square foot on these small production units, the access paths throughout the garden were only 10 inches wide, too narrow for wheelbarrow use. At this time the city of Paris was self-sufficient in fresh vegetables. Early writers referred to the Parisian fruit and vegetable growers as 'goldsmiths of the soil' who knew the exacting and intensive techniques to create exquisite vegetables through all the seasons of the year. One writer at the time explained how intensive vegetable culture differs from ordinary vegetable growing in the sense that "it needs to be a successive process uninterrupted during the year, often with many different vegetables planted together on the same piece of ground". This level of intensive year-round production was powered by at least 100 and sometimes up to 400 tonnes of horse manure per acre depending on how many hotbeds were used (decomposing manure provided the nutrients and organic matter and was also used to heat up the beds).

Text adapted from: Coleman, E. *The Winter Harvest Handbook. (2009)[13]*

Photo credit: *Archives communales de la Ville de Bobigny, near Paris*

Instead, I do as little as I can to spend as much time as possible with my children. We have a good quality of life. I'm 100% convinced that intensive micro-farms are a return to the future, as they allow producers to have a decent life and feed people healthily."[12] Québécois Jean-Martin runs a pioneering online marketing gardening course and this promises effective international exchange and learning about the important practice that is emerging from *the Jardins de la Grelimette[12.]*

The Yorkshire 2030 scenario above suggests that universities and businesses can together lead food research and training in a region's cities – realistic? Certainly there are existing models for such partnerships, one respected approach is the 'City Innovation District' pioneered since 2014 by the Brookings Institution in the USA[14].

Around the world the 'City Innovation District' is generating a lot of discussion between universities, business leaders and city governments. This urban innovation model moves well beyond conventional notions of 'science and innovation parks' to something much more strategic ie. compact geographic areas where 'anchor institutions' and companies cluster and connect with start-ups, business incubators and accelerators so as to share ideas and open innovation. There seems real potential for such Innovation Districts to help deliver economic value and social justice for cities through: important applied circular economy research relating to the city; professional development for private, public and commons sector leaders in the city; and university student entrepreneurship within the surrounding city region.

But perhaps this city innovation district model tends to be at risk of 'corporate capture'? Maybe a city government might be tempted to see only large corporates as the central anchor business institutions in the city. An example: a city plans to tackle its household and business food waste situation by inviting a company like Agriprotein (figure 50) to establish a large-scale centralised soldier fly factory that captures and monopolises say 90% of food waste flows in the city – rather than a more distributed 'leaky' nutrient-exchange model where numerous small scale distributed Agriprotein factories are established around the city. The temptation for the company and city government is to develop only the large-scale highly efficient and profitable enterprise. The small scale distributed approach is more challenging especially if the emphasis is to avoid the conventional notion of the small-scale factories then just scaling up to be deemed successful – instead, it's maybe more about developing a dense and long lasting (resilient) network of small and profitable soldier fly compost production enterprises that serve their local communities at urban district scale (alongside the larger-scale centralised Agriprotein factory?).

So perhaps something more radical than a 'city innovation district' is required for transformational change towards a distributed food economy for our cities? We've already talked about the importance of 'wise governance' for all this to work at scale... by providing an enabling macro-economic platform that resonates. Wise governance sets the overarching enabling conditions, then waits as it tunes in for the feedback before any adjustments to the initial enabling conditions.

A fundamental reassessment of the role of cities is currently playing out with the peer-to-peer (P2P) movement and its ideas around the 'city as Commons and Partner State'. Michel Bauwens, as one of the movement's leading theorists and practitioners, believes P2P theory can help us reimagine a new kind of state or city – one that directly empowers and enables civil society to be autonomously productive [15]. Tommaso Fattori [16] imagines how the re-emergence of the commons in our cities can ignite a grassroots economic development process where city residents "regain capability and power to make decisions, to orientate choices, rules, and priorities, re-appropriating themselves of the very possibility of governing and managing goods and services in a participatory manner: it is this first person activity which changes citizens into commoners"...

Stacco Troncoso[17] notes that the commons-based Partner State is most prevalent, and most feasible, at the city level:

"I think the city level is where the commons are most embedded at the moment. If you look at the experiences of Barcelona, Seoul...(or) the Co-Bologna experiment in Italy... these represent a poly-centric governance model where policy making is actually done at the grassroots level. It empowers citizens' groups to make policy proposals. I think this is very radical, even though it's also very pragmatic. Policy making is opened up to citizen collectives, while the city becomes an enabling mechanism to realise these projects......[and] cities cooperate in new ways through a new trans-local urban level that didn't exist before. So, for example, 40 cities worldwide have coalesced to regulate Uber......"

Kevin Carson, another respected theorist in the peer-to-peer/commons movement[18], believes that the goal for citizens is not just in policy-making but also in directly developing innovative projects and solutions – and that open source digital platforms can help realise the idea of the 'city as Commons' because the platforms can enact all sorts of other open source principles: low barriers to participation; transparency of process; bottom-up innovation; social pressure for fair dealing; and resistance to concentrated power and insider dealing. He argues that the key actors in building these new urban systems are "ordinary people acting as householders, makers, hackers, permaculturists, citizen-scientists, cooperatives, community foresters, subsistence collectives, social mutual lists, and commoners" – the city and national 'governments' should be merely supportive.

Stacco Troncoso discusses how Barcelona recently hosted an international Commons Collaborative Economies conference, which was focused on commons-oriented peer production and

Figure 52: Commons Collaborative Economies conference, Barcelona

Photo credit: PROCOMUNS

the collaborative economy[19]. This event issued a series of policy recommendations addressed both to the Barcelona municipal government and to the European Commission. It also focused on guidelines for building software platforms to support the collaborative economy. Barcelona has taken a small step towards the Partner State model with 'decidim.barcelona', a public collaborative platform for making policy proposals. Decidim ('we decide' in Catalan) allows the public to participate directly in government as they would a form of social media, and they have had early success.[19] The city council has hosted several organizing events to decide on a strategic plan, and nearly 40,000 people and 1,500 organisations contributed 10,000 suggestions. One of the functions Decidim supports is participatory budgeting, but there are many others. In 2020 there were over 1,000 active commons initiatives in Barcelona[19].

Within Barcelona, the Poblenou neighborhood of the city is leading a new urban model of resiliency and local innovation[18], where citizens are perceived not just as consumers but as producers, empowered through access to digital fabrication tools and knowledge. Poblenou is currently exploring how to step away from importing most things into the city and exporting waste, and instead introduce a circular economy model, where all material resources flow in biological and technical nutrient loops within the city itself. The city is already building the infrastructure to be locally productive and globally connected, in order to produce at least half of what it consumes by 2054. Poblenou is also a major participant in the FAB Cities network. The city council has successfully proposed turning a square kilometre of Poblenou into a 'Maker District' focusing on: fabrication and recirculating materials inside the city; food production through urban agriculture practices; and renewable energy production that utilises the latest solar technologies.

Kevin Carson[18] demonstrates that currently there is a wide variety of P2P initiatives in cities that illustrate small elements of a full-blown, commons-based urban economy. But the different parts are rarely seen together in the same place. What's needed, he says, is to integrate them into a fully evolved ecosystem of information and land commons, co-housing, community-orientated food enterprises, cooperatives, makerspaces, community workshops and co-working spaces. According to Carson, it's vital to share infrastructures to maximise the effective use of capital goods and reduce the need for ownership. And complimentary infrastructures are also needed for sharing or bartering skills like child care, local barter currencies, mutual credit, and so on.

But what a challenge all this is. How best to work with such approaches to develop ambitious urban food networks? The difficulties involved are recognised in Raychel Santoa's recent review[20] of the successes and limitations of urban food networks in the USA,

UK and other regions. For many urban food networks, fundamental questions have surfaced around establishing objectives. For instance, interviewees in Santoa's research discussed how many urban food networks have pursued low-hanging fruits, 'feel-good things' like farmers markets and healthy eating initiatives instead of more contentious, but also perhaps more transformative food system issues such as land ownership reform, labour rights, commodity subsidies and dietary recommendations. Competing discourses amongst food network members regarding what problems they seek to address and how to address them underscore more fundamental issues among urban food networks: what is their actual purpose or their strategy to transform food systems? Different answers require different actions and membership make up. For example, debate exists over what gives a diversity of stakeholders. Some view it as a cross-sectoral array of organisational representatives and decision-makers whereas others emphasise grassroots community engagement. Some aim to connect local food advocates with similar underlying values, while others urge the inclusion of 'conventional' stakeholders to achieve more widespread systemic (though maybe less progressive) change. The radical versus reformist potential of food networks has been debated for years[20], but these opposing approaches can create divisions within urban food networks and within the trans-local food networks connecting them, threatening their cohesiveness and capacity for transformative action.

Yet there are growing signs that civil society organisations recognise such limitations and are beginning to develop ways to progress more radical and strategic food systems change e.g. in England a consortium of well-respected organisations is currently collaborating on the development of *A People's Food Policy*[21] - organisations like Sustain, the Soil Association, the New Economic Foundation and the Land Workers Alliance (affiliated to La Via Campesina) have consulted and collaborated with a wide range of interests. Their vision for the English food system:

"There is strong democratic control and participatory governance over our food system. Food and farming policy-making includes the active participation of a vibrant and politically engaged civil society...Everybody, regardless of income, status or background, has secure access to enough good food at all times...Land is recognised and valued as an essential resource for food and shelter and the basis for numerous social, cultural and spiritual practices. Land is no longer treated and traded as a commodity; instead, it is understood as a common good of the people...People's values and perceptions have shifted to support a more democratic and diverse food system... Food is still traded internationally but is not treated simply as a commodity ripe for speculation...This is a food system which guarantees everybody's right to food, that protects and regenerates our land, rivers and seas, and pays people fairly for the work they do."

In future, top of the agenda must be the issue of how to engage diverse cultural and socio-economic groups in urban and peri-urban agroecology and food sovereignty issues. The process of engagement and capacity building within such groups is a priority although finding facilitators and educators with those invaluable capacity building skills is perhaps one of our biggest challenges. To address this, a recent Nesta report *Our Futures: By the People, for the People* details the exciting potential for so-called 'futures participatory techniques'. 'Deliberative democracy' and capacity building is critical, it's back to those 'schools of democracy' again.[22]

The need for a systemic approach to a regenerative urban food economy is illustrated at the end of this chapter (figures 54). Some observations. Firstly, this illustration hints at 'nutrient infrastructure' in this urban and peri-urban food system: biological materials matter very much and are a potential source of value if 'waste can become food'. Yet, for us, the richness doesn't come from an urban materials economy *per se* but from a shifting kind of economic development and food system that takes advantage of the *distributed circulation and exchange* of materials along with the regeneration of natural and social capital, the circulation of value, the circulation of money city-wide, the development of skills and having access to resources, tools and infrastructure which are capital building.

Figure 54 indicates the critical role of the private sector. As observed by Olivier de Schutter and Jose Luis Vivero Pol, at the heart of a regenerative food model needs to be a radically reformed private sector: "there is an urgent need to build a different breed of private enterprises that thinks beyond the bottom line of profit motivation. This transformed private sector needs to be driven by a different ethos, making profit, yet bound by requirements to contribute to social aims and the satisfaction of the needs of the community."

There is a growing recognition internationally of this need to shift private enterprise beyond just the profit motive. An important new report from the British Academy and Said Business School at Oxford University[23] considers how it is only in the last 60 years that corporate purpose has come to be equated just with profit. That's been damaging for corporations' role in society, trust in business and the impact that business has had on the environment, inequality and social cohesion. Such issues highlight the need for a rethinking of the corporation around its purposes. The British Academy report[23] explains that in earlier times, corporations were originally established with clear public purposes:

"Throughout its 4,000-year history from the Code of Hammurabi in Babylonia, through the Roman Republic to the East India Company and the Industrial Revolution, business enterprise has been motivated by a strong element of public purpose[24]. It is only

Figure 53: Diverse business ownership models are needed in the food system. Riverford is an employee-owned UK business with 650 people, sharing 80% of profits. Turnover of £60 million with 50,000 boxes of fruit and vegetables/week[25]

Photo credit: Riverford

over the last 60 years that the drive to equate corporate purpose with increasing profit has become so acute...(yet) the purpose of corporations is not to produce profits. The purpose of corporations is to produce profitable solutions for the problems of people and planet. In the process it produces profits, but profits are not per se the purpose of corporations........ [And] the ownership of corporations is currently associated with shareholdings. That is a mistake and leads to an inappropriately restrictive conception of ownership. Instead, ownership should primarily be related to the formulation and implementation of corporate purpose. There are many forms of ownership that are associated with this including individual, family, institutional, employee, cooperative, mutual and public ownership, depending on the nature of corporate purposes. This points to the importance of diversity of ownership and the responsibilities as well as rights that go with it."

Figure 54 shows the importance of the commons-based sector in urban food systems. New commons forms and practices are needed, including in our food systems. There is a need for new types of federation among commoners and linkages between different tiers of commons. Thus to realize the food commons and deter their market and state enclosure, we need innovations in law, public policy, commons-based governance, social practice and culture. All of these will manifest a very different worldview than that which now prevails in established governance systems, particularly those of the State and Market. Building the food commons and associated commons infrastructures means enabling or creating resources which are primarily governed by their users – these suit the smaller operations without much capital and are low cost or replicable. Examples include platform cooperatives where the commons is the software, such as the Open Food Network software now available internationally[2]. In physical spaces, the whole commons infrastructure around community land trusts, food stores, use of municipal lots for food enterprises, community kitchens etc. can have a very strong sense of being managed by the users rather than the state or market.

This illustrative urban landscape reminds us of the Partner State relationship with both the commons-based and private sectors: the Partner State is about making opportunities available rather than deciding how the urban and peri-urban private sector and food commons are developed. The role here for the state is to connect up an ecosystem of regenerative farming tools and enterprises to ensure, if possible, the cascading flows and exchanges of biological materials and energy within the distributed networks and nodes of these complex private sector and commons-based systems. A vital role of enabler governance here is to make sure the monetary 'capillary beds' (the blood analogy again) do their job and enhance the *exchange* function and build value with what the communities of commoners and entrepreneurs already have.

Figure 54 hints that a transformed private sector with a new sense of purpose needs to engage directly with commons-based organisations – social enterprises, cooperatives, employee-owned businesses in themselves are of course so valuable but there is added value when private sector business organisations engage with the commons sector itself e.g. private owners of large farms ensure that at least a small portion of their land has strong commons access and user rights and is available for commons-orientated enterprises and infrastructure.

The idea of revisioned private enterprises is picked up nicely by Sebastien Parsons with his so-called 'Commons Corporation'[26]. His particular emphasis is on the for-profit enterprises nested within the regenerative food network and his commons corporation model, clearly influenced by the biomimicry work of Janine Benyus, focuses on networks of enterprises, nested systems, flows of money, cycles and dynamic balance. His idea of a Commons Corporation offers a new economic model that is a contribution towards solving the profit maximisation obsession without inhibiting entrepreneurial activity or private ownership. Through new organisational design we can refocus the energy of the market into making business regenerative rather than extractive of value from people, place and environment. A Commons Corporation is an economic ecosystem of privately owned enterprises and commons/civil society organisations, legally associated, that provides mutual benefit both for those organisations, the individuals within those organisations and also the host communities of which they are a part. It is a new type of mutual economic structure that binds companies and commons/civil society organisations together in a way that protects and develops shared value. As such it is a systemic contribution to building a new kind of 'self-regulating capitalism' and commons ecosystem. The Commons Corporation is distinct from other mutual business organisations such as co-operatives or single social enterprises or even community benefit societies because of its systemic approach. Unlike employee-owned companies that simply distribute and consume/use their surplus (e.g. John Lewis in the UK), a Commons Corporation is a systemic enabler for change because its inherent structural logic invests in the commons through built in processes for scaling out and stability[26].

Finally, figure 54 indicates this is all about a diverse and distributed network of food enterprises which provides a thriving base, adding value to what is already available and that is able to *scale out* (rather than *scale up*). Each network is adjusted to local circumstances. Like dividing cells in the body, these urban and peri-urban food enterprises need to scale out into a network by propagation and replication. Cell growth is nourished by surrounding nutrients from the blood – likewise small enterprises are nurtured by the circulation of spending in the local economy. To thrive, these smaller businesses need to see key public and private institutions circulating spending within their reach – perhaps regional or community banks, access to universal basic dividend and investments on infrastructure and tools from which to build. A regional bank is suggested in the illustration. That's because in the typical regenerative food system the small and medium sized food enterprises in the commons-based and private sectors are often unable to draw down commercial capital and need to resolve the ongoing dilemma of having enough customers to thrive while large scale business extracts value from the region.

A few concluding comments: around the world new regenerative food production systems, tools and ideas are flourishing – but not yet at scale. So many more people want to participate in a regenerative food economy yet system conditions constrain their involvement. This is primarily because, so far, the underlying macroeconomic narrative and distributed food economy infrastructure has been so slow to develop. It's difficult to imagine large-scale participation in a reinvigorated food democracy without widespread access to tools, resources, infrastructure and effective income and currency. This is where the role of city governance and the Partner State comes into play – there's a crucial need for 'wise governance' in our cities, a willingness to enable urban food economies to thrive at macro, meso and micro scales...it's about a city government enabling a transformative circular economy using the shorthand of *Circular Economy=1x2x4/4* (chapter 1). For regenerative food and farming systems in and around cities, it's all about government setting the enabling conditions for: effective stocks, flows and exchanges of biological nutrients; regeneration of soil; enterprise stacking; and development of business enterprises with 21st-century purpose.

STATE/MARKET/COMMONS DYNAMIC

State: role of partner state to enable creation of loosely coupled and decentralized infrastructure, then observe how this infrastructure affects the 'coupling', the feedback - then adjust accordingly.

Market: revisioned private sector with 21st century purpose. Diverse food business types and sizes e.g. apple and honey co-operatives, community interest companies, share farms. Commons: secure access and user rights e.g. on common grazing land, ocean commons, community orchards, allotments.

COMMONS INFRASTRUCTURE/ ORGANISATIONS

Reinvigorated democracy and food sovereignty through participation in diverse food commons organisations e.g. community kitchens, local open source seed banks, temporary food stores including chill/refrigeration, regenerative agriculture tools library.

NUTRIENT INFRASTRUCTURE

Value creation/distribution from biological materials e.g. large/small sized soldier fly plants and biogas/composting facilitiess using kitchen waste (unpolluted nutrients returned to regenerate soil in surrounding market gardens)[29,31]

MONEY FLOWS AND EXCHANGES

Smaller businesses thrive as key state and private institutions circulate spending within their reach e.g. regional banks, access to universal basic dividend, 'beetroot bond', capital investments for regenerative food infrastructure/tools.

BUSINESS MODELS

e.g. enterprise stacking for value creation/ distribution on regenerative farms and market gardens.

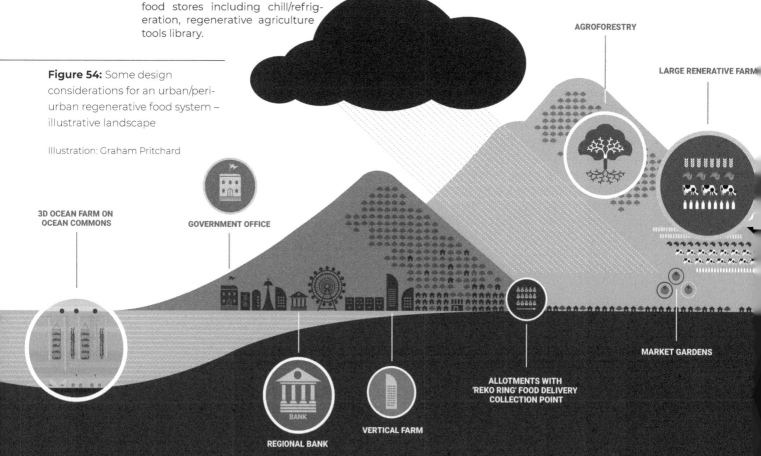

Figure 54: Some design considerations for an urban/peri-urban regenerative food system – illustrative landscape

Illustration: Graham Pritchard

AGROFORESTRY

LARGE RENERATIVE FARM

3D OCEAN FARM ON OCEAN COMMONS

GOVERNMENT OFFICE

MARKET GARDENS

REGIONAL BANK

VERTICAL FARM

ALLOTMENTS WITH 'REKO RING' FOOD DELIVERY COLLECTION POINT

DIGITAL REVOLUTION
e.g. online food produce markets such as 'REKO rings' and Open Food Network[30] for regenerative food enterprises and networks.

EFFICIENCY-RESILIENCE BALANCE
e.g. large supermarkets and smaller-scale nested markets of regenerative food producers/ retailers (scaling out into distributed networks by propagation and replication).

DIETS
Balance of vegetables, fruits, nuts, pulses, fungi, meat, dairy etc. for healthy diets – this guides design of regenerative food production/processing systems.

DIVERSITY OF REGENERATIVE FOOD SYSTEMS
e.g. market gardens, mixed farms, allotments, 3-D orchards, agroforestry[34], 3-D ocean farms, 'vertical farms'/aquaponics[33], small/mobile abattoirs, smokeries, mobile dairies.

BIODIVERSITY
e.g. rewilding of landscape[32].

MEASURES OF SYSTEMIC HEALTH
See figure 41 in chapter 4 for details.

LEARNING
e.g. bridging networks, regenerative food research between producers/retailers/universities/government and commons organisations.

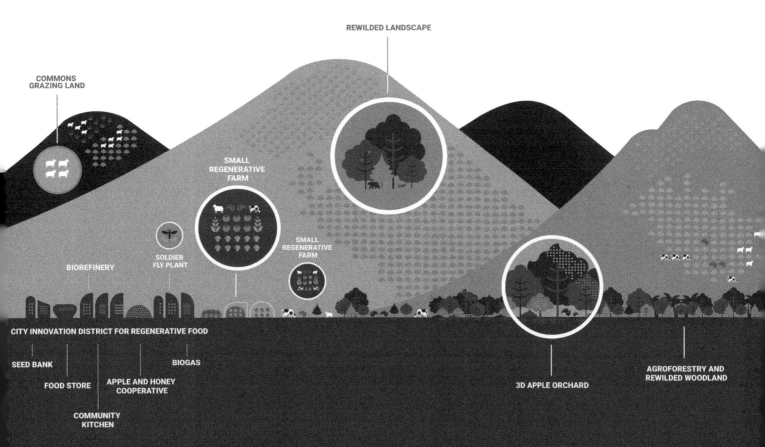

REWILDED LANDSCAPE

COMMONS GRAZING LAND

SMALL REGENERATIVE FARM

SMALL REGENERATIVE FARM

BIOREFINERY

SOLDIER FLY PLANT

CITY INNOVATION DISTRICT FOR REGENERATIVE FOOD

SEED BANK

FOOD STORE

APPLE AND HONEY COOPERATIVE

BIOGAS

COMMUNITY KITCHEN

3D APPLE ORCHARD

AGROFORESTRY AND REWILDED WOODLAND

And working alongside this enabler government is both a commons sector and a radically restructured private sector, with business organisations of many sizes with diverse ownership types and structures. This is about a revisioned private sector with motivations beyond profit...businesses orientated around the biomimetic principle of 'competition+cooperation=dynamic balance'. When the private sector works closely with commons organisations and enabler governments, the sort of networks of organisations that then emerge start to sound like George Monbiot's transformative 'bridging networks'[27]. Then there are those important questions for urban and peri-urban bridging networks. How might small(er) scale production thrive in food networks so that it contributes to soil regeneration and better food (and diet) for people? How important is affordability of food? What if we could free up people's enterprising spirit, what does that take and what would then happen in the food enterprise networks?

For us, what's clear is that this approach needs to be one of evolution, tryout, feedback and adaptation with a rigorous commitment to critical thinking and experimentation through the active involvement of universities, business, government and commons organisations within the city region. There will be successes and failures but out of this experimental mix can emerge a wealth of regenerative, accessible, distributed and abundant urban food solutions.

References and notes for chapter

1. Steel, C. *Hungry City.* Vintage (2013). Also see.her new book *Sitopia*. Penguin Books. (2020)

2. See for example Open Food Network https://www.openfoodnetwork.org

3 *Our Future in the Land. Food*, Farming and Countryside Commission. RSA. (2019). Beetroot bond reference on page 26

4. Ramos, J., Sweeney, J., Peach, K. and Smith, L. (2019). *Our futures: by the people, for the people. How mass involvement in shaping the future can solve complex problems*. NESTA

5. Moore, R. (2018). A blueprint for British housing in 2028. *The Observer*

https://www.theguardian.com/artanddesign/2018/jan/21/blueprint-for-british-housing-2028-not-utopian-dream

6. Food affordability enabling conditions: see chapter 1 of this book for four monetary principles in a transformative circular economy

7. Craig Johnson pers.comm. Neil Marshall, Director at Growing with Grace organic market garden. July 2020. This figure relates to unheated greenhouses with a March to October growing season in a northern temperate climate www.growingwithgrace.org.uk

8. A new type of solar cell is coming to market. *The Economist.* Article on perovskite crystals

https://www.economist.com/science-and-technology/2018/02/03/a-new-type-of-solar-cell-is-coming-to-market

9. Insect farming. AgriProtein website and BBC radio programme featuring Jason Drew, AgriProtein's CEO https://agriprotein.com/ and https://www.bbc.co.uk/sounds/play/w3csv0pk

10. The International Platform of Insects for Food and Feed (IPIFF) promotes the use of insects and insect derived products as an important source of nutrients for animal feed and human consumption www.ipiff.org

For protein production from fly larvae also see: Pauli, G. and Kamp, J. *Plan A. The transformation of Argentina's economy.* JJK Books. (2017)

https://www.argentina.gob.ar/sites/default/files/plan-a_the-transformation-of-argentinas-economy.pdf

11. Low Impact Living Affordable Community – Leeds LILAC. 2020

https://www.lilac.coop/

12. Details on the *Jardins de la Grelimette* in *No Time to Waste: The Rise of a Regenerative Economy* by Guibert del Marmol and Joanne Maguire-Charlat. Ker. (2017)

Jean-Martin Fortier's regenerative market gardening book: http://www.themarketgardener.com/

13. Coleman, E. *The Winter Harvest Handbook.* Chelsea Green. (2009)

14. Katz, B. and Wagner, J. (2014). *The rise of Innovation Districts: a new geography of innovation in America.* Brookings Institution

https://www.brookings.edu/wp-content/uploads/2016/07/InnovationDistricts1.pdf

Bruce Katz TEDxHamburg 2015 https://www.youtube.com/watch?v=8ou-bkgjVN4

https://www.brookings.edu/research/positioned-for-growth-advancing-the-oklahoma-city-innovation-district/

15. Structured bibliography of P2P and Commons by Ira Mollay and Michel Bauwens. 2019

Good section on urban commons.

https://wiki.p2pfoundation.net/Structured_Bibliography_on_P2P_and_the_Commons

16. Tommaso Fattori biography https://wiki.p2pfoundation.net/Tommaso_Fattori

17. Stacco Troncoso, Finding Common Ground 6: Constructive confrontation or constructive tension – The State and the Commons. *P2P Blog*, January 2, 2017

18. Carson, K. (2017). *Libertarian Municipalism: networked cities as resilient platforms for post-capitalist transition.* Centre for a Stateless Society.

19. Utratel, A.and Troncoso, S. *The Commons Collaborative Economy Explodes in Barcelona.* (2018) http://commonstransition.org/commons-collaborative-economy-explodes-barcelona

Also see:

https://decidim.org/demo/

and the map/directory of commons initiatives in Catalonia/Barcelona

https://procomuns.net/en/resources/commons-map-of-catalonia/

20. Santoa, R. and Moragues-Fausb, A. (2019). Towards a trans-local food governance: Exploring the transformative capacity of food policy assemblages in the US and UK. *Geoforum* 8

Also see the article *What should the next generation of urban food policies look like?* by Albane Gaspard of Urban Food Futures. (2020) https://urbanfoodfutures.com/2020/05/21/next-generation/

21. *A People's Food Policy: transforming our food system* (2017)

https://www.peoplesfoodpolicy.org/download

22. *Our Futures: By the People, for the People.* NESTA. (2019) https://www.nesta.org.uk/report/our-futures-people-people/

Also see the authoritative OECD guide on 'deliberative and participatory democracy': *Innovative citizen participation and new democratic institutions: catching the deliberative way.* OECD Publishing. (2020)

https://read.oecd-ilibrary.org/governance/innovative-citizen-participation-and-new-democratic-institutions_339306da-en#page1

23. *Reforming business for the 21st century: a framework for the future of the corporation.* The British Academy. (2018)

https://www.thebritishacademy.ac.uk/sites/default/files/Reforming-Business-for-21st-Century-British-Academy.pdf

Also see this valuable discussion from Nick Hanauer and Eric Beinhocker on the role of business in a redefined capitalism

https://www.mckinsey.com/featured-insights/long-term-capitalism/redefining-capitalism#

24. "The corporation was established In Roman Law to perform public functions of minting coins, collecting taxes, looking after public buildings and undertaking public works. It was then used in the governance of municipalities in Europe, the creation of the first universities and the establishment of the Roman Catholic Church. The corporation was also the basis of the emergence of the merchant trading companies, most notably the East India Company, and then the companies that built the railroads and canals. With freedom of incorporation in the 19th century came the private company, which was the backbone of the rise of manufacturing industry, service companies and transnational corporations. It is only over the last 60 years that the drive to equate corporate purpose with increasing profit has become so dominant." Source: *Reforming business for the 21st century: a framework for the future of the corporation.* The British Academy. (2018)

25. Butler, S. (2018). Staff ownership ensures organic veg firm Riverford doesn't forget its roots. *The Observer* https://www.theguardian.com/business/2018/apr/07/riverford-organic-veg-employee-ownership-plan

26. Sebastian Parsons presentation on the Commons Corporation. He is chief executive of Stockwood Community Benefit Society https://www.youtube.com/watch?v=x7nnxxZ66jI&feature=youtu.be https://stockwoodcbs.org/ Also see Sebastian Parsons at Oxford Real Farming Conference 2020 https://soundcloud.com/user-775591787/orfc20-cc-13-farm-succession (audio from 10.30)

27. Monbiot, G. *The new political story that could change everything* TED Summit 2019. 'Bridging networks' at 13.00 in the video https://www.ted.com/talks/george_monbiot_the_new_political_story_that_could_change_everything?language=en

28. Jacobs, J. *Cities and the Wealth of Nations.* Random House. (1984)

29. Reports with comprehensive coverage of urban strategies for value creation with biological material cascading. See for example: *Cities and Circular Economy for Food* (Ellen MacArthur Foundation, 2019) https://www.ellenmacarthurfoundation.org/assets/downloads/CCEFF_Full-report-pages_May-2019_Web.pdf

and *Circular Amsterdam: a vision and action plan for the city and metropolitan area* (Circle Economy, 2016) https://issuu.com/fabrications/docs/circular-amsterdam-en-small-210316_

30. Presold produce from online food markets such as 'REKO rings'. Originator of REKO is Thomas Snellman. Good video and map of over 500 REKO rings in Scandinavia. Demo map of REKO rings at 6.20 in this video https://www.youtube.com/watch?v=NfdJ4678olQ&feature=youtu.be

31. Bio-manufacturing plants are also key in urban nutrient infrastructure e.g Biohm and Ecovative Design https://ecovativedesign.com/__https://www.biohm.co.uk/regenerativemanufacturing

32. Rewilding Europe aims to create large, rewilding landscapes across different regions in Europe

www.rewildingeurope.com

33. Despommier, D. *The vertical farm: feeding the world in the 21st-century.* Thomas Dunne Books. (2010)

34. See United Nations FAO agroforestry definitions: http://www.fao.org/forestry/agroforestry/

CHAPTER 7

...AND D IS FOR DEMOCRACY

"To create a minimum standard of life below which no human being can fall is the most elementary duty of the democratic state".
Walter Lippman, *Drift and Mastery*[9]

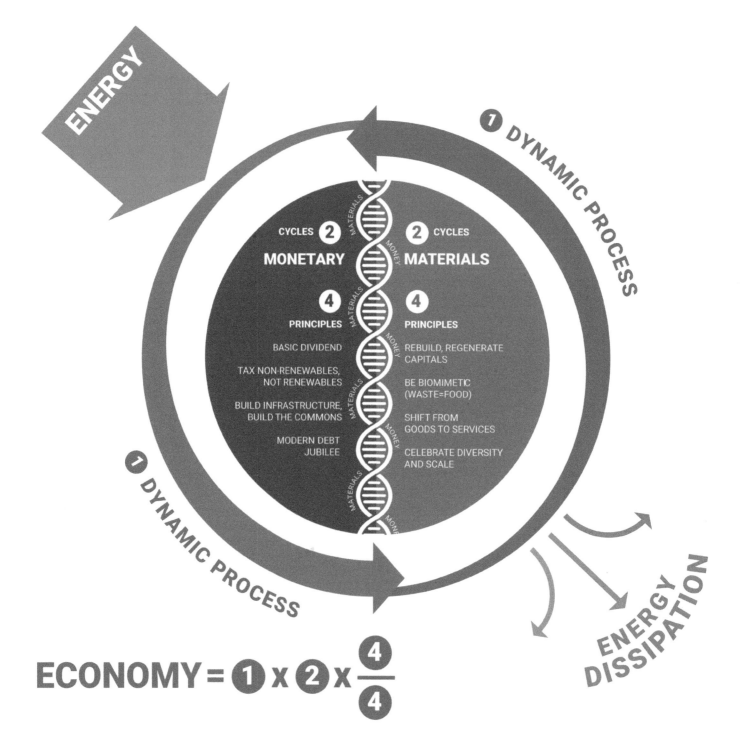

ENERGY

① DYNAMIC PROCESS

① DYNAMIC PROCESS

CYCLES ② ② CYCLES

MONETARY MATERIALS

④ ④

PRINCIPLES PRINCIPLES

BASIC DIVIDEND

TAX NON-RENEWABLES, NOT RENEWABLES

BUILD INFRASTRUCTURE, BUILD THE COMMONS

MODERN DEBT JUBILEE

REBUILD, REGENERATE CAPITALS

BE BIOMIMETIC (WASTE=FOOD)

SHIFT FROM GOODS TO SERVICES

CELEBRATE DIVERSITY AND SCALE

ENERGY DISSIPATION

$$\text{ECONOMY} = ① \times ② \times \frac{④}{④}$$

In a way, the rationale for the exploration in this book has been to offer 1x2x4/4 as a structure for an economy which better integrates resource questions with money cycles. It's a heuristic, a pointer towards a progressive future: it suggests that the circular economy is about rebuilding capitals through the shift from extraction to circulation, in monetary and materials cycles *simultaneously*. They are symbiotic, to use a living systems perspective. The aim is to create an economy which is regenerative, accessible and abundant, by design.

After all, this is about a systems perspective around 'circularity' and it is pretty intuitive. That same systems approach also prompts the recognition that economies of scope and diversity are just as important as economies of scale – 3-D orchards and 3-D ocean farms are a reflection of that too – adding value to what we already have and building capital, not degrading it. And this book also makes the case that it's a useful change of perspective to see economics more from the standpoint of gardeners than engineers, to take Nic Hanauer's metaphor – it's that complex living systems perspective again (box 6).

All this weaves in and out of probably the most important context of all and that is a participative democracy. Aspects of this were central to the discussion of food systems in cities (chapter 6). Society depends on the environment, the functioning ecosystems, for sure. But how we react effectively to multiple examples of climate and biodiversity crises depends ever more on having a resilient means of decision making which is adapted to us as economic and social (citizen) participants – not as supplicants or dependents. Ultimately, we believe that a reinvigorated democracy is our only defence and the only source of support and hope that will make sense, as we experience the sharp reality of the non-linear changes ahead.

Figure 55 (opposite page): A transformative circular economy

Illustration: Graham Prichard

BOX 6

MARKETS AS MACHINES
VERSUS MARKETS AS GARDENS

Understanding economics in this new way is a shift from a tradition that prizes fixity and predictability, to a mindset that is premised on evolution.

Machine view: *Markets are efficient, thus sacrosanct*

Garden view: *Markets are effective, if well tended*

Complexity science shows that markets are often quite inefficient, but it also shows that markets are the most effective force for producing innovation, the source of all wealth creation. The question, then, is how to deploy that force to benefit the greatest number.

Machine view: *Regulation destroys markets*

Garden view: *Markets need fertilizing and weeding or else are destroyed*

Traditionalists say any government interference distorts natural markets, but complexity economists show that markets get overrun by weeds and exhaust their nutrients if left alone.

Machine view: *Income inequality reflects unequal effort and ability*

Garden view: *Inequality is what markets naturally create and compound, and requires correction*

Traditionalists assert, in essence, that income inequality is the result of the rich being smarter and harder working than the poor, but complexity economists believe income inequality has much more to do with the inexorable nature of complex adaptive systems like markets to result in self-reinforcing concentrations of advantage and disadvantage.

Machine view: *Wealth is created through competition and by the pursuit of narrow self-interest*

Garden view: *Wealth is created through trust and cooperation*

Where traditionalists put individual selfishness on a moral pedestal, complexity economists show that norms of unchecked selfishness kill the one thing that determines whether a society can generate wealth and opportunity: trust.

Machine view: *Wealth = individuals accumulating money*

Garden view: *Wealth = society creating solutions*

One of the simple limitations of traditional economics is that it can't really explain how wealth gets generated. Complexity economics says that wealth is solutions: knowledge applied to solve problems. Wealth is created when new ideas emerge from a competitive, evolutionary environment. In other words, money accumulation by the rich is not the same as wealth creation by a society. Our focus should be on making sure everyone has a fair chance – in education, health, social capital, access to financial capital – to create new information and ideas. Extreme concentration of wealth kills prosperity in precisely the same way that untended weeds overrun and then kill gardens. Equality of opportunity, then, isn't just a moral imperative – it is an economic imperative.

Source: *Liu, E. and Hanauer, N. The Gardens of Democracy. Sasquath Books. (2011) A synopsis by Craig Weightman* [1]

This sort of economy is hardly recognisable today and the simple representative democracy around two parties and their 'class' interests is equally strange and disconnected. Polity has fragmented. If we are talking democracy then it has to be a democracy for our times, not 50 years past or how we imagine it in a sort mythical way. Just as we can be uncomfortable with these old capital/labour/government and representative democracy scenarios there is also something very inadequate about Samuelson's simple diagram of our complex economy.

But, on the other hand, the Hudson and Bezemer diagram[3] has been a touchstone. Through them, we have discovered (chapter 1) that there are two major but somewhat obscured forces at play in the economy which are directly relevant to the discussion around democracy and its shape now and in years to come. The two forces are Money/Finance and Real Estate/Monopolies – the FIRE economy (Finance, Insurance and Real Estate, figure 57). These are not new but typically seem to have been grouped and hidden under 'Capital'. That's because they are seen to be as either much the same kind of animal as a factory, foundry or retail corporation or because they are seen as facilitators and intermediaries, in the case of money and finance. In truth, Hudson and Bezemer say these forces are distinct and represent property or, to be more precise, the ownership or enclosure of different kinds of 'commons'.

A commons is, as the name suggests, held in common. It is a resource and has a community of users. We argue that since money is 'fiat', a social contract or agreement, created by instruction (by 'fiat'!), money too can be seen as a commons, or at least a public utility – usable by all. Money is essential, both as a medium of exchange and powerful as credit. Whom does it serve? The rights to create and inject money is a kind of monopoly – charging interest on it is a form of rent seeking. No longer does money even require at least some effort to obtain as a commodity – gold or silver for example. Equally, the

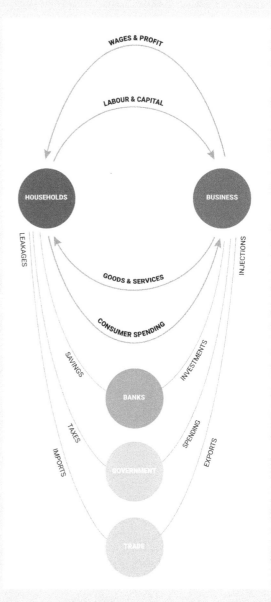

Figure 56: Simplified visualisation of an economy

Based on: Paul Samuelson[2]

Illustration: Graham Pritchard

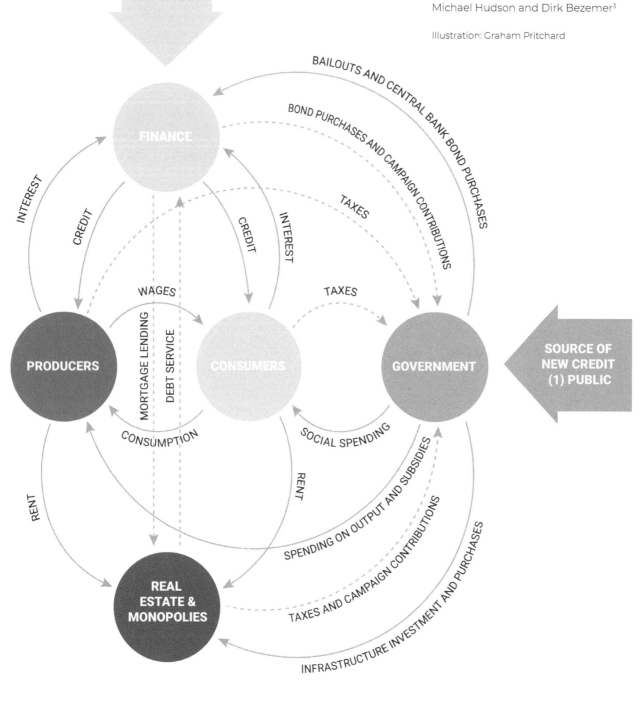

Figure 57: The FIRE economy After Michael Hudson and Dirk Bezemer[3]

Illustration: Graham Pritchard

ownership of real estate, intellectual property or rights to use parts of the electromagnetic spectrum is very powerful, as indeed are shares, including second-hand shares in companies which separates ownership from day-to-day control. Ownership of assets represents various forms of enclosure of the commons: land; the right to issue money or create credit; the right to access technologies that are protected by patents; and so on. From this follows the debate about where to levy taxes or fees; in which of the cycles or which stocks and which flows shown in the Hudson and Bezemer illustration? At present, this is overwhelmingly done via income and consumption taxes rather than on resources, energy, capital gain or land value (see figure 56). In many ways, this is just an artefact of the social narrative which grew up over time, first into the mid 20th century and then in a changed form into the 1980s-present day. That narrative was around wealth creators needing to retain profits or dividends for the purpose of further wealth creation and thus economic growth.

In the foregoing discussions we made the same point as many earlier writers that there is a tension; an interplay between the productive economy and the non-productive one, the latter mostly consisting of unearned income or rents on assets that have been enclosed. The owners receive a payment for allowing access to an asset. It is the reward 'to property not activity'. This all has a long history. In the view of Hudson and Bezemer, and others like Steve Keen, these hidden or obscured sectors – they call them the FIRE economy – should be brought into the limelight once again. The overall system can then be understood better as a result. In this book, the idea of things like fossil fuel resources, land, IP, the right to create credit and the exploitation of digital commons (e.g. data contributed to social media or our personal information) – are all given as examples of forms of enclosure. This creates a dividend, a return to ownership. Hence our argument that in a reinvigorated democracy it is very important that this dividend should be shared between the enclosers and all those citizens who have rights to obtain benefits from the commons (the world's 'common-wealth'). In this way, everyone becomes a 'rentier' because with the establishment of a universal basic dividend everyone then has a share in the commons. Perhaps it starts with shareholdings for all employees or in ways that Guy Standing has outlined[10].

Society is in a very long running debate about how the 'commons' should be treated. History tells us – from the 1930s Great Depression or the Gilded Age in 1890s in the USA or even the fall of Rome – what happens when the interests of the non-productive sectors dominate the productive. Inequality expands and the productive economy is starved of its lifeblood. Indeed, the driving notion of Manchester Capitalism and other forms of *enterprise*-orientated approaches in past centuries were originally about readjusting this relationship. Trade, exchange, factory production and the limited liability corporation was seen to be superior and far more beneficial than the dead hand of landlord and the banking institutions. Free enterprise indeed, free from the control of the vested interests of the time.

Economics in the classical era, from its inception in the 18th century and through to the late 1890s was deeply concerned with how to understand the relationship between capital (as in working or productive capital), labour and land. It is perhaps disappointing that this changed in the neoclassical period when land was grouped and hidden under Capital - thus the debate was 'simplified'. This was done deliberately, according to the late Mason Gaffney[4], as a direct response to the last great assault on the non-productive economy in the latter part of the 19th century, in the USA in particular. At this time, Henry George, whose books sold in the millions, was shining a light on the contradiction between rapid material progress and the existence of poverty. He argued that the 'rentier' was the person/group that was benefitting. In the classical tradition it was the factor called 'land' which was getting the benefits. But if land is no longer visible as a category in the economic model and instead fits under capital then the wind goes out of George's sails - to criticise capital means criticising enterprise. In parallel, there was a deep-seated unease about the way restrictions on the supply of currency were damaging the economy as it grew. (from 1873 in the USA it was linked to gold). There was a movement in the USA to go back to using silver too and as William Jennings Bryan said[5] in a famous speech in the Democratic Convention of 1896:

"Having behind us the producing masses of this nation and the world, supported by the commercial interests, the laboring interests, and the toilers everywhere, we will answer their demand for a gold standard by saying to them: "You shall not press down upon the brow of labor this crown of thorns; you shall not crucify mankind upon a cross of gold."

So it's clear that the fault lines of that period and perhaps of our own time is properly between Hudson and Bezemer's non-productive FIRE economy and the productive economy. That's because these fault lines expose the question about the choice between circulating value more than extracting it and retaining it or, as we have discussed, placing it into a money to money cycle of its own.

The inadequacy of the existing democratic tradition then becomes clearer. It was as if the shift described in this book – from centralised to complex adaptive, that we see everywhere in the real world of systems – was to be ignored and the myths of labour versus capital maintained. Making the democratic choice between the devil of the 'free' markets of capitalism and deep blue sea of overwhelming State control looks meaningless. Why, we say, in a digital world, is there so much intermediation, so much control via the large digital corporations, when we can be more networked and connect in different, more fluid and specific ways? In a way, figure 58 asks how democracy might work in the situation at the bottom right-hand side of the illustration.

Perhaps this could be summarised in the following way. The democratic challenge is no longer one of monolithic blocks of people contesting different 'class' interests once in a while with a shared but erroneous view of what changes can be made to an economy. Instead, the tussle is increasingly between productive and unproductive economy, between participation and being a supplicant, between complex, multiscale involvement and token representation at fixed moments. It's not capitalism versus communism or markets versus states. It is not even enterprise versus rentiers if we are all also due a dividend from the productive use of the commons, which in turn enables enterprise of all kinds. Enabling enterprise at multiple scales speaks of more opportunities for 'schools of democracy' and a positive cycle then comes into sight. "Whom does the economy serve?" Is answered by "all of us" but in new and more nuanced ways. But these ideas are as ancient as the Babylonians and world religions when the periodic debt jubilees and injunctions against loans at interest were designed to reset the balance between the asset owners and 'toilers' and to relieve the latter of a burden lest the economy become moribund. This kind of active management of the economy is quite the opposite of much of the mythology of the moment which says 'keep a balanced budget' and once every five years use the democratic process to argue about the level of state spend and tax on income and consumers. It is a misdirection. What is more central to the democratic discussion is how productive and unearned income interests oscillate. The important question is does the FIRE economy dominate or not? Finance and the rentiers led in the Gilded Age – which led to the Progressive Era in USA in the 20th century - and once more dominated in the post-World War 1 financial boom of the 1920s which led to the Great Depression. The struggle between industrial and financial interest led into a very dark period of authoritarianism before the post-war settlement after World War 2 – and where its principal architect Maynard Keynes looked forward to the euthanasia of the rentier. It was not to be.

But the resilience required for these ecologically-disrupted times speaks of more than the oscillation between productive and non-productive: the added dimension is that of rebuilding or reimagining the role of the commons at many scales – and regenerative capitalism by the by, as the stories around 3-D apple orchards and 3-D ocean farms reveal. This book has sought to re-orientate the way we see the economy to include Money/Finance and Real Estate and Monopolies, but also to recognise the existence of multiple nested, fractal scales. And because of this, new forms, or potential forms, of democratic expression are required – lest we lose democracy itself.

We need to build commons. In two parallel myths, in the USA and in Central Asia, there came a person, a selfless but distant character, who planted apple tree seeds in advance of when they were needed in order to create a commons, a resource for the

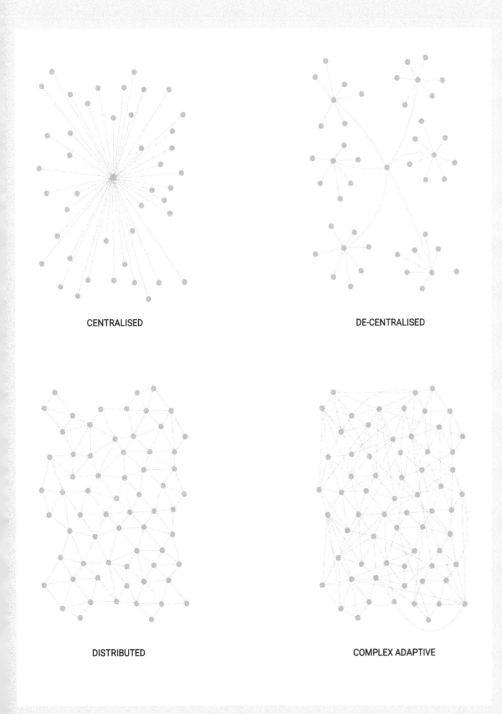

Figure 58: Centralised, decentralised, distributed and complex adaptive systems

Adapted from: Paul Baran[6]

Illustration: Graham Pritchard

CENTRALISED

DE-CENTRALISED

DISTRIBUTED

COMPLEX ADAPTIVE

Figure 59: John Chapman (1774-1845), better known as Johnny Appleseed, was an American pioneer nurseryman who introduced apple trees to large parts of Pennsylvania, Ontario, Ohio, Indiana and Illinois

Credit: MarkauMark / Shutterstock.com

future (figure 59). That character then faded out of the picture but the legacy endured – the apple orchard as an archetypal example of enhanced production and bounty. In our own times, the question is also focussed around the digital commons. We contribute every day and yet the bulk of the benefit goes elsewhere.

Like all such 'commons', the resource is managed by its users, it is not a wild place, a 'jangal' – the Hindi word for uncultivated ground and our 'jungle'. And the commons are not a 'tragedy' – as Garrett Hardin[7] would have us believe – since they only become a tragedy of overexploitation when the rules of the community disappear, often because the community of 'commoners' has been removed or overwhelmed. It is commoners who carefully manage the commons resources, through time and seasons, by balancing what can be harvested against what needs to be preserved and by identifying those times when new investment and new rules are needed – this is what underlies the skill to be human. Surely we are reciprocators as well as interested in ourselves, collaborative as well as competitive. And the notion of justice and fairness and the long term surely has much to do with deciding how to manage a commons. It was, after all, the group rather than the individual that usually powered human evolution; social relations have always been paramount. Within these discussions and debates are some of the roots of the idea of devolved decision making. Although not formalised, it is the needs of the community of users which nowadays needs different kinds of democracy, participation and being fair to all.

Equally, history is full of examples where there are people who would enclose the commons, and divorce the ownership from participation. Through ownership, they seek to acquire the surplus or its value and would deny access to a share of the output of an enclosed commons or make access conditional on appropriate service or even demand it through enslavement or, through its near neighbour, feudalism. The proposal that rights of property

are superior to human rights is such an ancient trope or idea that it has been central to power struggles for thousands of years. Its form keeps changing but the essence is that enclosed property confers power and those without property are not part of the decision making process, because they have no stake in the management of that property. If you own nothing then you are nothing. All you have to sell is yourself, for a wage. But in earlier times you obtained permission to work some enclosed land, or earn your freedom by service to the state, often in the military.

It was only much later, as feudalism broke down, when land and property ownership spread, that a newer class of property owner also joined those with rights to be involved in decision making. That is the paradox in a way. Property conferred the right to make decisions. This group grew larger and so only much later was the voting franchise extended to workers, and then only males (since the marriage gave the 'ownership' of the wife to the man) and then finally to females. This legacy is a huge weakness if it slips into the trope, the simplistic rationalisation, that those with property still deserve more respect, more protection from the law. In most countries the laws around property are far stronger than those around the person. Try to be a tenant or a welfare recipient, or homeless or even face a court bailiff to experience the difference.

Hence the idea of the universal basic dividend from the commons. As a first stage, some of this might come through the entitlement of workers to shares in private companies so that the prosperity from 'enclosure' is manifestly shared through dividends. Or it might be one step removed, via a citizens' wealth fund. Economist Mark Blyth and Eric Lonergan describe such a shift in the book *Angrynomics*[11] Indeed, there are a number of competing ideas about how to build a strong base to the economy. This might be a job guarantee or universal basic services – both of which might be closer to state provision while dividends or a universal basic income might be more individually focussed, the state more of an intermediary or supplier of funds.

'Every One Every Day' is an example of how, even if we can find a way of channeling income to the base, it needs to work along-side the provision of infrastructure to enable diverse enterprises to flourish (figure 60). We've illustrated how small scale enterprises like 3-D orchards and 3-D ocean farms can add considerable value, as well as serving the needs of carbon sequestration, social resil-ience and exchange (chapter 4). For a reinvigorated democracy, we have argued for a levelling of the playing field for enterprise by shifting taxes away from people and onto non-renewable resources (e.g. oil, minerals). And we require a shift from private debt creation for real estate (and other assets) into lending for productive activity, that enterprise network, so as to enable the new infrastructures of renewables, mobility, food and housing.

This need is easily recognised in figure 61 which displays the example of UK bank lending to different sectors earlier this century. It was overwhelmingly about lending to the FIRE sector and still is. This must surely be re-orientated, and since the ability to create money as credit is a privilege given to banks it can also be circum-scribed by lending guidance from the central bank. Then, add in money as a public utility via the other money creation point (see figure 57) and ensure that we are not being governed by fixed or

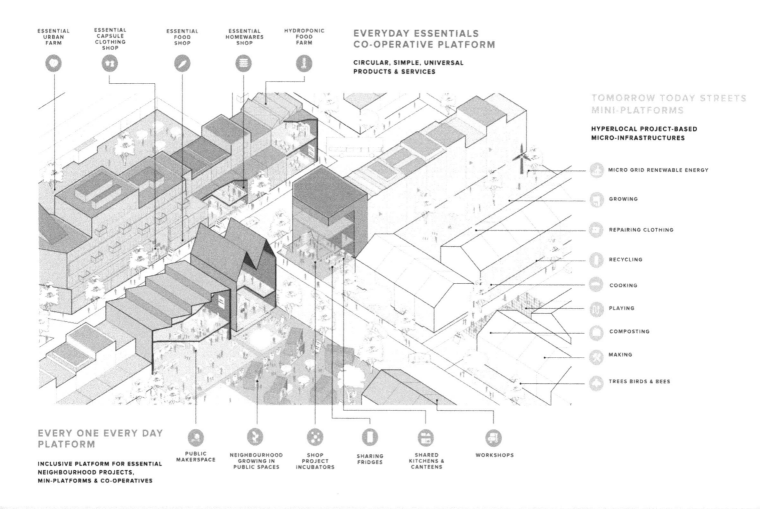

Figure 60: 'Every One Every Day' – a platform for local people in Barking and Dagenham (London) to build their neighbourhoods together, combat social isolation, and strengthen their communities. Adding value with what is around us

Credit: Tessy Britton/ Participatory City Foundation/Every One Every Day[8]

balanced budgets. Instead the emphasis, in future, must be on the degree to which new money increases production and consumption and human wellbeing without raising prices, and doing what is necessary, anyway, to adjust to the climate crisis and build an infrastructure that is, not by coincidence, entirely consistent with the aspirations in this book.

In short, a reinvigorated democracy is about the potential for people to participate in creating their own wellbeing and to make decisions which matter – from our perspective, this comes from the basis of a security and confidence of having a basic dividend (it's their entitlement and for the respect this brings).

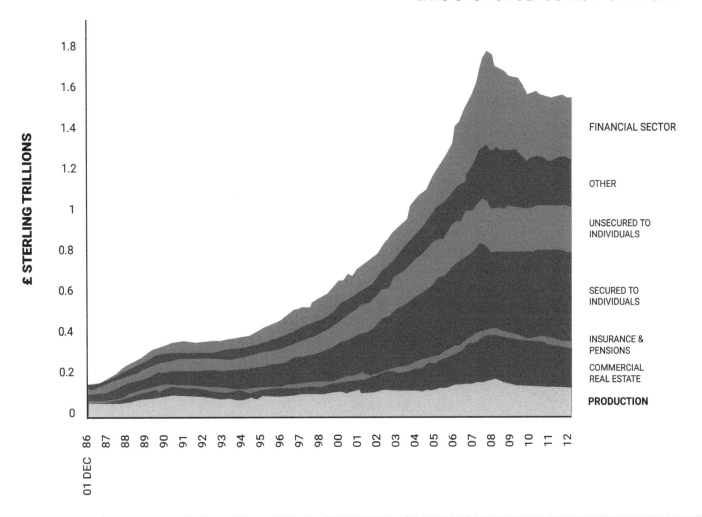

£ STERLING TRILLIONS

FINANCIAL SECTOR

OTHER

UNSECURED TO
INDIVIDUALS

SECURED TO
INDIVIDUALS

INSURANCE &
PENSIONS

COMMERCIAL
REAL ESTATE

PRODUCTION

All this needs to be set within an enabling macroeconomic framework and an inclusive, contemporary and scientific worldview. It is simply not enough to tweak existing policies, to 'do less harm.' The context brings meaning after all and that is what is missing right now – the narrative. Plato insisted: 'Those who tell the stories rule society'. But whose stories will succeed? We are at risk, as Nesrine Malik said[12] after the Trump inspired insurrection in 2021: "we are drowning in an ocean of political failures, but we don't talk about the water."

Figure 61: UK resident bank lending by sector 1986-2013 Source: Bank of England

Illustration: Graham Pritchard

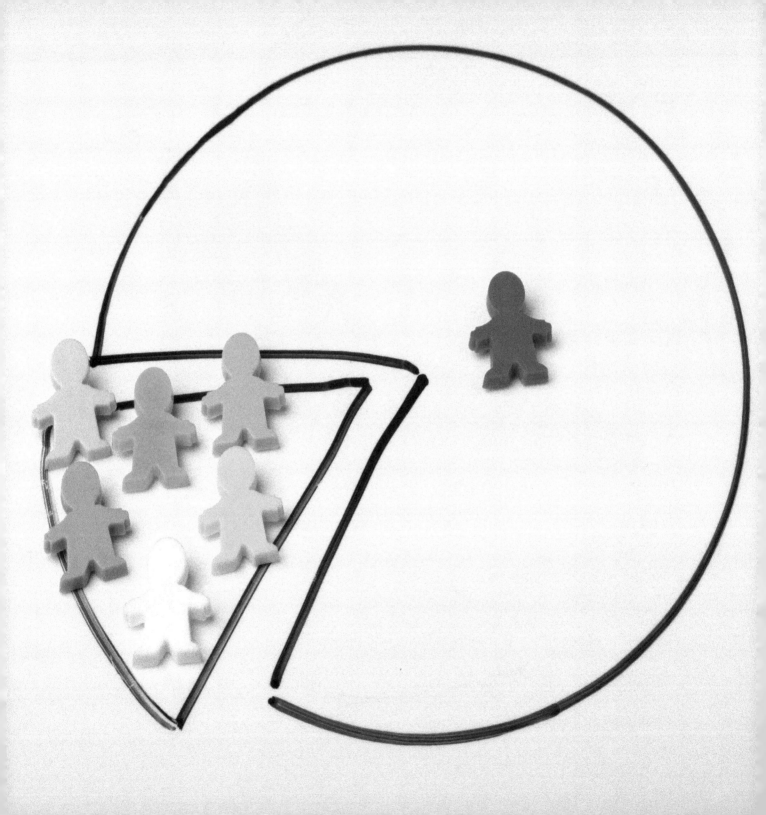

Chapter references and notes

1. Liu, E. and Hanauer, N. *The Gardens of Democracy: A New American Story of Citizenship, the Economy, and the Role of Government.* Sasquath Books. (2011)

A synopsis by Craig Weightman https://www.everyday-democracy.org/sites/default/files/sites/default/files/Gardens-of-Democracy-Summary.pdf

2. Samuelson, P. *Economics.* McGraw-Hill. (1948)

3. Hudson, M. and Bezemer, D. (2016). Finance is not the Economy. Reviving the conceptual distinction. *Journal of Economic Issues*, 50, pp.745-768

https://www.boeckler.de/pdf/v_2016_10_21_hudson.pdf

4. Mason Gaffney https://www.masongaffney.org/vita.html

5. William Jennings Bryan speech to the Democratic Convention of 1896

http://historymatters.gmu.edu/d/5354/

6. Baran, P. (1964). On distributed communications. Memorandum, August 1964. The Rand Corporation

https://www.rand.org/content/dam/rand/pubs/research_memoranda/2006/RM3420.pdf

7. Hardin, G. (1968). The tragedy of the Commons. *Science,* 162, pp.1243-1248

8. Britton, T. *Universal basic everything: creating essential infrastructure for post-Covid 19 neighbourhoods.* Participatory City Foundation/Every One Every Day (2020)

https://medium.com/@TessyBritton/universal-basic-everything-f149afc4cef1

9. Lippman, W. *Drift and Mastery: an attempt to diagnose the current unrest.* University of Wisconsin Press. (1914)

10. Standing, G. *Basic income: and how we can make it happen.* Pelican. (2017)

11. Lonergan, E. and Blyth, M. *Angrynomics.* Agenda Publishing. (2020)

12. Malik, N. (2021). The lesson of the second wave is that we must demand lasting political change. *The Guardian*

https://www.theguardian.com/commentisfree/2021/jan/11/second-wave-political-change-global-pandemic

Craig Johnson

From 2010 to 2017 Craig was Higher Education Programme Manager at the Ellen MacArthur Foundation where he worked with university partners on the development of circular economy -oriented courses and professional development resources. Craig is an ecologist with a particular interest in food sovereignty issues and the development of regenerative agriculture and horticulture enterprise networks in urban and peri-urban settings. Craig is currently a consultant and lives in the Yorkshire Dales (UK).

Ken Webster

From 2010 to the end of 2018 Ken Webster was Head of Innovation for the Ellen MacArthur Foundation and helped synthesise contemporary understanding around the 'circular economy'. Ken is currently based in Wales and makes regular contributions to conferences and seminars around the world. His current interests include open vs closed circular economy approaches, regenerative agriculture and integrating the monetary and materials stocks and flows. He is currently Visiting Fellow at Cranfield University, Director for the International Society for the Circular Economy and member of the Club of Rome's 21st Century Transformational Economics Commission. This volume is the latest in a series of cooperative projects developed with Craig Johnson over several decades beginning in 1986 and including co-authoring Sense and Sustainability (2008).